CALENDAR

CALENDAR
Christ's Time for the Church

Laurence Hull Stookey

Abingdon Press
Nashville

CALENDAR: CHRIST'S TIME FOR THE CHURCH

This book is printed on acid-free, recycled paper.

Library of Congress Cataloging-in-Publication Data

Stookey, Laurence Hull, 1937–
    Calendar: Christ's time for the Church/Laurence Hull Stookey.
      p. cm.
    Includes bibliographical references and index.
    ISBN 0-687-01136-1 (pbk.: alk. paper)
    1. Church year.   2. Time—Religious aspects—Christianity.
 I. Title.
 BV30.S73   1996
 263'.9—dc20
                                                      96-382
                                                     CIP

Unless otherwise indicated, scripture quotations are from the New Revised Standard Version Bible, copyright © 1989, by the Division of Christian Education of the National Council of the Churches of Christ in the United States of America. Used by permission.

Those noted RSV are from the Revised Standard Version of the Bible, copyright 1946, 1952, 1971 by the Division of Christian Education of the National Council of Churches of Christ in the USA. Used by permission.

00 01 02 03 04 05—10 9 8 7 6 5 4

MANUFACTURED IN THE UNITED STATES OF AMERICA

In Memory of
Clarence Curtis Goen
July 4, 1924–December 26, 1990

Revered Teacher, Scholar, and Sage
Esteemed Colleague
Treasured Friend
Beacon to Heaven

CONTENTS

PREFACE

Even the most casual perusal of the table of contents will reveal that there is something very odd about this book. The season of Easter is discussed before the season of Lent, which is (as everyone knows) quite backward. Worse yet, both Easter and Lent are considered ahead of Christmas, and Christmas is discussed before Advent. All of this might seem the result of some gross mishandling of computer data, not caught by uncomprehending copyeditors. On the contrary, it is quite deliberate and springs from a basic theological assumption about how the story of Jesus (and the liturgical calendar that springs from that story) can best be understood.

For this is a book primarily about the theology of the calendar. It does not repeat the excellent research of scholars of the history of the calendar such as Adolf Adam, Marion J. Hatchett, and Thomas J. Talley. And unlike the first two volumes of this trilogy (*Baptism: Christ's Act in the Church* and *Eucharist: Christ's Feast with the Church*), this book is not primarily a compilation and popularization of material well known to serious students of the subjects but too technical or scattered to be readily accessible to others. This work ventures into waters more uncharted. Note well its scope as *a* theology of liturgical time, not *the* theology of liturgical time. Many alternative interpretations of the calendar are possible, and I hope that the limitations of this study will goad others into providing a more competent consideration of what is begun here.

Calendar is intended not only for clergy and those preparing for vocations within the church but also for laity who wish to understand more fully the core of the Christian faith as expressed week by week in worship. I hope that within these pages both those who preach and those who teach within the parish will find insights that clarify their thinking and enliven their tasks.

11

The substance of the book is divided between basic text and endnotes. The notes contain material that is either a bit esoteric or somewhat to the side of the principal discussion. I advise most readers to ignore the notes until finishing each chapter, or even all of the chapters. Those who cannot bear to face immediately the strange arrangement already noted (and those who read the last pages of mystery novels first) may want to begin their reading with the "cheat sheet"—appendix 2, on forgetting what you were always taught.

This book has been more than twenty years in the making, frequently shunted to the side by projects that were more pressing or seemed better to finish first. Hence I cannot remember all who have contributed to my thinking, which has changed many times across those decades and will continue to change after this is in print. But in the final stages of the writing I have relied heavily on the advice and aid of a host of people: My faculty colleagues who have read portions or all of the manuscript, particularly Professor James C. Logan and Dean M. Douglas Meeks; another faculty colleague, who assisted me in translating word processing programs, Dr. David C. Hopkins; my faculty secretary, Veronica Boutte, who has been a superb proofreader as well as general assistant; and Mordena Millar and Anna St. Aubrey Stookey, who helped to read page proofs.

In 1960, when I was a student at Wesley Seminary, there came to the faculty a young professor of church history, Clarence Curtis Goen. Later we would serve as faculty colleagues for fifteen years, on occasion team-teaching a course on the history of preaching in America. C. C., as he was known to many outside the seminary, came from a Southern Baptist heritage and upon arriving at Wesley knew little of the liturgical calendar save for the observances of Christmas and Easter. But in his three decades (as he liked to say) doing missionary work among the United Methodists, those Wesleyans had a perceptible effect upon him; for he developed a deepening respect for matters liturgical. His fine sense of history enabled him both to appreciate the observances of the calendar and to contribute to their significance in our worship. Clarence's untimely death shortly after retirement in 1989 was a great loss for the seminary, the community, and the church; yet even in his dying, he was our teacher. For twenty-nine years he taught us how to live as Christians, and for his last eighteen months he taught us how to die as Christians. Therefore to him this book is affectionately dedicated and all royalties are donated in his memory to the All Saints Chapel Fund of Wesley Theological Seminary.

PROLOGUE

Many moviegoers must have left the theater scratching their heads at the end of *Places in the Heart.* For its final scene is full of puzzles. A congregation is gathered for worship; attendance is rather sparse. As the pastor reads about love from 1 Corinthians 13, Wayne and Margaret Lomax, recently estranged by his infidelity, begin to hold hands. (A moment before, his lover and her husband have been shown leaving town for a new home in another city, thus signaling the end of the illicit affair.) Then the elements of Holy Communion begin to be passed amongst the congregation; Wayne and Margaret receive the sacrament together. How nice. And may they all live happily ever after!

But as the bread and wine are passed from person to person, suddenly the congregation is more numerous than before. Where did these people come from all of a sudden? Some of them are indeed the villains of the plot. At length the sacramental trays are passed to the pew in which earlier there sat only Edna Spalding, her two children, and Mr. Will, her blind boarder. But now sitting next to Will, at one end of the pew, is Moze, the African American who enabled Edna to prevent foreclosure on her small farm by bringing in the crop of cotton. Two things are strange about his presence. First, in an earlier scene he had said his good-byes to Edna, and fled town under threat from the Klan. Second, even had that not happened, it cannot be imagined that any African American would be accepted into a white congregation in Waxahachie, Texas, in 1935, let alone as a welcome communicant. What is going on here?

Moze receives the sacrament and passes it on to Will, who in turn gives it to Edna's children, Possum and Frank. Edna herself receives and passes the tray to her husband, Royce. Whoa! He was murdered within five minutes of the opening of the movie, shot in the line of

15

duty as sheriff by Wylie, an inebriated African American youth. What is Royce doing in church at the end of the movie? With the words, "the peace of God," the deceased sheriff passes the sacrament to the person next to him, who turns out to be none other than his slayer. Wylie then receives communion, saying to Royce, "The peace of God." The strange scene fades slowly from the screen as the movie closes.

But the questions pile up. How did a small congregation become large? How is it that African Americans and white Texans are in the same congregation in an era of immense racial conflict? How are the dead to be found among the living? How can a murderer and his victim exchange "the peace of God" with each other? It makes no sense.

So is it to be regarded as sheer fantasy—the ultimate fairy tale ending? Not from a Christian perspective. From that vantage point something else entirely is going on. But to understand what is occurring, we must consider the strange nature of time and the way in which Jesus Christ transforms that time for the church. It is this task to which we now turn.

1

Living at the Intersection of Time and Eternity

To be deeply Christian is to know and to live out the conviction that the whole human family dwells continuously at the intersection of time and eternity. A superficial Christianity may be content with far less, believing merely that some portions of the human family dwell there—for example, only those who are "believers," as defined, perhaps, very narrowly. Or a superficial Christianity may identify certain occasions on which God, the Eternal One, has momentarily entered into human history or into the experience of particular persons, only to be obscured again thereafter. But such interpretations of the Christian faith fail to grapple with the way in which God is perpetually at work in all of creation.

The abiding conviction that history and eternity continuously intersect is grounded in the most basic of Christian affirmations. For our scriptures insist that in the days of the Emperor Augustus the eternal Word of God became flesh and dwelt among us, born in Bethlehem when Quirinius was governor of Syria. Further, our creeds affirm that this Christ—"God from God, Light from Light, true God from true God"—was crucified in the time and under the jurisdiction of Pontius Pilate and rose from the dead after three days. To take these assertions seriously is to be bound to the conviction that God and human history are intertwined.

Hence, as Christians we *ought* continuously to be aware that we live at the intersection of time and eternity, but often we are not; for one thing, our preoccupation with the pressures and demands of time itself obscures the presence of the Eternal One in our midst. The poet Wordsworth complained that "the world is too much with us; late and soon, / Getting and spending, we lay waste our powers." Since his day nothing has changed to decrease our penchant for ignoring God in the face of life's pressing demands. But oblivious-

17

ness toward God is only part of the story; the rest is that often God prefers to work incognito, hidden away from public acclaim. Was God any less at work in our midst during nearly three decades in a Nazareth home and carpentry shop than during the brief months of Jesus' public ministry in Galilee and Judea? This is a question theologians rarely address, but one that has profound implications for our understanding of how God labors among us.

Holy hiddenness is neither a punishment from God nor a denial of grace to us. It is a gift. Luther, it is said, at the end of the afternoon frequently would invite one or more of his coworkers to join him in a time of relaxation. But his excessively conscientious associate, Philip Melanchthon, frequently tried to prevent this on the grounds that "there is too much work that we need to be doing to reform the church"—to which Luther would reply in exasperation, "Philip, *God* is at work even while we are drinking beer." God's hidden labors in our midst should allow us to live faithfully without the stultifying intensity that takes us to the brink of self-idolatry by causing us to believe everything of importance depends on us, and us alone.

Still, at times our natural preoccupation with the pressures and details of life and the holy hiddenness of God produce a negative result: Time obscures the very eternity it is intended to reveal. For this reason Christians have found it helpful—even necessary—to keep track of time in special ways that call to remembrance God's work among us. Once each week we observe a day of worship; this all Christians of every age and place have agreed upon, even if they have had some disputes about whether this should occur on Sunday to commemorate the resurrection (as most assert) or on Saturday to give thanks for the completion of creation (as "seventh day Christians" insist). Then there are annual observances to remind us of God's acts in our midst. Christmas, Easter, and Pentecost are familiar to all Christians; to these, many others add observances of Advent, Epiphany, and Lent. Most churches set aside certain days on which to recall the work of Christ's grace in the lives of the faithful departed, whether or not they officially designate such persons as saints. In some traditions even hours of the day are designated to call to remembrance our encounter with God in Christ: noon in commemoration of Jesus hanging on the cross, three in the afternoon to mark his death, and evening to commemorate his sojourn in the sepulchre; dawn to recall the discovery of the empty tomb, and midnight to proclaim the Lord's return when least we expect it.

That Christians should find it useful to observe seasons, days, and hours in ways that make evident the eternal in our midst may seem eccentric until we reckon with how essential time-keeping is in organizing human experience. Imagine trying to navigate your way through life with no access to a clock or calendar of any kind. Utter disorientation would result. In recent times a number of persons have been held hostage under such conditions of deprivation. For extended periods of time, they have been denied the slightest glimpse of sunlight, and so could not even determine when day ended or began. Terry Waite expressed the confusion and frustration common to them all:

> I have spent about four days in the underground prison—at least I think it's about four days. The guards won't tell me the time, and I can only guess the hour from when they come to take me to the toilet and bring me food. . . . The thing I find most worrying is not being able to measure the passing of time. If I am to keep myself together, I must find some means of doing this.[1]

One form of social control imposed on American slaves was to withhold from them the dates of their birth; thus Frederick Douglass took great pains to try to discover his birth date, in order that thereby he might know who he was. As those who hold hostages or slaves know all too well, human identity and functioning are utterly dependent on time-keeping. Is it odd, then, that Christians find spiritual time-keeping to be so crucial to their identity and action?

Time: Past, Present, and Future

Coming to terms with the relationship of past, present, and future is crucial to an adequate theology of time. For the most part, we think of these as distinct categories, isolated from one another as if in separate containers. In diagram form the usual assumptions look like this:

PAST	PRESENT	FUTURE

The present in this understanding is a significant duration of time, which may vary from person to person or occasion to occasion; but usually when we talk about "the present" we mean the current decade or century, or, perhaps, events within our own lifetime or slightly beyond. "The past," by contrast, refers to what may fall into the category "history." And "the future" refers to what is well beyond experience. Given this boxed-in view of past, present, and future, the present is given the greatest value. The past often is viewed at best as the preliminaries ("The past is prologue.") and at worst as something superseded ("What's past is past.") or utterly irrelevant ("History is bunk."). In the same way the future also is often distanced from us. "Don't live in the future," we are warned; "you have to deal with things as they are now. Nobody knows what tomorrow holds." Because the visions of heaven and the end of time have been so abused by certain kinds of religious fervor, in church circles the hope of the future may even be dismissed as false: "Pie in the sky when you die, by and by." Thus the future hope cherished by many people of faith is suspected of being an escape from the demands of the present.

Because the Bible abounds with stories about the past and the future, the model just illustrated alienates us unnecessarily from biblical ways of thinking. Consider a model quite different:

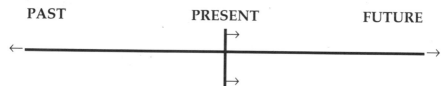

In this understanding, time is a continuum, not a series of boxes. The present is but the moving edge between the past and the future. In some sense the present barely exists. This should not suggest that the present is unreal or unimportant, but only that it is always a moving edge of the thinnest sort. In a moment you will read a word set in all capital letters; your reading of that word is now a future event. BUT now your reading of that word is a past event. In this understanding of things, the past is far more than prologue and the future far more than a distant dream. The present cannot be conceived in isolation, as if it had a life of its own. Always the past, present, and future are of a piece.

20

That the past shapes the present seems the less controversial of the assertions. We know from experience that we are inheritors of much that we possess, all the way from the gene pool, which helps to determine who we are as persons, to the national debt, which helps to determine how much we as citizens have to pay in taxes. We are only beginning to realize how much we suffer from past abuses of nature, leaving us with polluted streams, radioactive landfills, holes in the ozone layer, and depleted forests. On the other hand, in thousands of ways of which we are only dimly aware, we are the benefactors of the labor and sacrifices made by those who went ahead of us.

It may be less evident, however, that the future also shapes us in important ways. Theologians call this shaping power of the future "eschatology" (literally, "the things at the end"); but one need not be a theologian in order to have an eschatology. As I was growing up in mid-America during the post–World War II years, a compelling eschatology had gripped the nation. There were ominous reports of the massive military power of the Soviet Union, and FBI director J. Edgar Hoover and Senator Joseph McCarthy were finding fifth-column communists in every crevice. The possibility of a thermonuclear holocaust was discussed daily in the media. The future, in short, seemed to have the shape of a mushroom cloud.

The effect upon the present was horrendous. Inordinate sums of money were spent on defense. Air-raid sirens, installed in every community, were tested periodically, so that no one could ignore their presence—or the impending doom they prefigured. School-children were routinely put through civil defense drills, and yellow-and-black signs everywhere indicated the location of bomb shelters. The affluent built private bunkers in their yards, and sometimes stocked them not only with food and water but with guns and ammunition to ensure that no one outside of the family would intrude in time of panic. As a preteen, I worried whether my little village in Illinois was far enough from St. Louis to escape devastation when the Russians would (inevitably, it seemed) send their missiles hurtling over the North Pole at a city that had a lively munitions industry. And suppose their aim was bad and they hit my town directly! Not many called this view of things an "eschatology"; but that is precisely what it was. *Life* magazine photographs of Hiroshima and Nagasaki haunted us, as the past conspired with the future to shape the present in terrifying ways.

To live as if the present could be boxed off from the past and the future is unrealistic even for someone who has no concern for religious thinking. But for Christians, rooted in biblical traditions, the task is doubly untenable. The Christian story reaches back to the Exodus of ancient Israel and before and stretches forward to the descent of a new heaven and a new earth and beyond. Indeed, it can be said that Christians are called to assume a cruciform posture: Standing upright with feet firmly planted in the present, we stretch out one arm to grasp our heritage and the other arm to lay hold of our hope; standing thus, we assume the shape of our central symbol of faith: the cross. If either hand releases its grip, spiritual disaster threatens as the sign of the cross becomes misformed.

Eternity: Divine Humiliation-Exaltation and the Cross

The cross is the key not only to the Christian faith but also to the definition of eternity as we consider its intersection with time. For the cross reveals the humiliation-exaltation that is a distinctive characteristic of the Eternal One.

It must be emphasized at the beginning that the defining movement of humiliation-exaltation is not an innovation that begins at Bethlehem or shortly before. We Christians see this divine movement most clearly in the presence of Jesus in our midst; but always God has been and will be working this way in the world in order to be made known to the fullest extent that the divine *can* be understood by humanity.

Therefore it is well to rid ourselves of misleading vocabulary, particularly that which speaks of Jesus as "God's intervention into history."[2] Such language suggests that God was inactive, perhaps even uninterested, in the history of the world until a certain point at which drastic action became advisable or necessary. But what kind of God is it who creates a world and then walks off, becoming a passive observer until some crisis occurs that seems overwhelming? No, the Creator is ever active in the creation; but at points that activity is less obvious to humanity than at other times. The contrast is not between a God who is here and a God who is absent, but between the work of God that is sometimes obvious and sometimes hidden.

Two models by way of illustration: (1) In ancient Greek drama, often a playwright would allow the human situation to get into such a tangled mess that all hope seemed lost. Then, at the bleakest point in the play, seemingly from out of nowhere, a chariot would appear and in it a deity. That divine being, who until this point had not interacted in the plot, would magically reconcile all differences and set everything right. Because the deity arrived on stage in a mechanical conveyance, this technique came to be known by the Latin phrase *Deus ex machina*, literally, "God from the machine."

(2) By contrast consider a handwoven tapestry depicting lush vegetation. Looking at the right side of the tapestry, the eye sees primarily a vast expanse of green intertwining vines and leaves. But every now and again there appears a small yellow bud—not yet a full bloom, but only a bud. In contrast to the dominant green of the fabric, these yellow patches are scattered: subtle occurrences in the overall pattern. But turn the tapestry over and behold on the other side the vast maze of threads that create the design. Suddenly, the yellow, so scarce on the upper side, is everywhere. Indeed the underside may seem predominantly yellow, for the golden threads not woven into the upper design continue underneath, unbroken from the point of one floral bud to the next.

God's activity in the world is better thought of as the yellow threads of that tapestry than as a *Deus ex machina* drama. God is not a Creator who stands outside creation and intervenes only when nothing else will be effective. Divine involvement is interwoven through human history—is always there, but more often than not unseen unless we turn history over and look at its underside. Thus what happens in Jesus Christ is not some surprising innovation, concocted in dire circumstances to provide emergency relief. What happens in Jesus Christ is the making evident of what God has ever been doing in hidden but purposeful activity. In other words, time and eternity continuously intersect; that is how God designed it. And though sometimes we are oblivious of that intersection, at other times we are made aware of it.

Suppose that, in the tapestry we have envisioned, the yellow buds are so small they could almost be lost to the eye of the casual observer. But in the visual center of the design the weaver has set one bud that has blossomed into full flower. That blossom, far from detracting from the many tiny patches of yellow throughout the tapestry, by its brilliance gives greater place to those subtle buds, ensuring that they will not be overlooked. In the tapestry of history, in which God is ever active even if often hidden, that central, brilliant blossom is Jesus Christ, who enables us to see so many other evidences of God's presence, and who causes us to know that God is always with us, even when hidden from view.

The manner in which this God works is clarified in the story of Jesus. At Christmas, we are made aware of the humility of a God who wills to be found in a feed trough. John Donne had this in mind when he entered the pulpit of St. Paul's Cathedral, London, on Christmas Day, 1626, and began his sermon this way:

> The whole life of Christ was a continual passion. Others die martyrs, but Christ was born a martyr. He found a Golgotha (where he was crucified) even in Bethlehem, where he was born. For to his tenderness then, the straws were almost as sharp as the [crown of] thorns after, and the manger as uneasy at first as his cross at last. His birth and his death were but one continual act, and his Christmas Day and his Good Friday are but the evening and the morning of one and the same day.[3]

Donne rightly perceived that humiliation characterized the incarnation from end to end. But humiliation implies dignity, for only the exalted can be humbled; and deep humiliation implies grandeur. If we are not struck by the humiliation of Bethlehem, perhaps it is because we have a deity who is too domesticated, made too much in our own image, though a bit bigger! But what if God, instead of being a larger version of ourselves, is quite apart from us—not alien (let alone unapproachable), but wonderful beyond our capacity to comprehend?

Imagine a scene in heaven before Bethlehem. God has convened a solemn council of all the heavenly host and now addresses them: "Despite our best efforts to be made known through creation, hardheaded humanity has not gotten the point. They do not understand divine love at work among them and rebel against it at every opportunity, often in the most vicious ways. Since they do not see

24

the grace we continuously pour upon them, we must make our activity more clear to them. If they are to be saved from themselves, it will be necessary for someone to go there from here, to take on human form, to reveal in person what we intend creation to be. Who will go for us?" There is a great silence in heaven. The angels stand on one foot and then the other, declining eye contact with one another. Each feels a sense of obligation but an utter unwillingness to take on the onerous task of dealing with humanity. Then comes the voice of God again: "Who will go for us? Who is willing to try to make more clear the message of heavenly grace to people caught in their own selfishness? Which of you will take on flesh and be born in their midst?" Another great embarrassed silence follows. Once again: "Who will go?" No one stirs. No sound can be heard. A fourth time God speaks: "Then I myself will go." In one accord the angels gasp. And then for an hour there is a silence greater than all that preceded, as the hosts of heaven grapple with the implications: God will go? God will take on flesh and walk among that vicious lot? Suppose those mortals, thinking this divine visitor to be merely one of their own kind, take up arms and do what humanity has done to one another ever since the time of Cain and Abel! It is a thought too amazing to be tolerated. No, they must have misheard what God said to them.

Herein lies the deep humiliation of God: that time and eternity have intersected in a way so obvious; that the Eternal One has been born in the days of Caesar Augustus and slain under Pontius Pilate, thereby sanctifying the whole of human history in all its sordid dimensions. The cross is the testimony that this is true. The cross is the verification that God has appeared in human flesh, condescending to accept agony and execution.[4]

The cross is also, however, the verification of the exaltation of God. How is it that the symbol of capital punishment in the Roman Empire has come to adorn church steeples and to be worn around our necks or on our lapels? How is it that an instrument of cruelty and torture has come to be made of gold, ornately wrought and encrusted with jewels of every sort? This is possible only if the humiliation of God is also somehow the exaltation of God. To such an odd confluence of meanings the New Testament testifies eloquently. In John's Gospel Jesus declares: "And I, when I am lifted up from the earth, will draw all people to myself" (12:32). The form of that lifting up, or exaltation, cannot be understood apart from an earlier statement in the same Gospel: "Just as Moses lifted up the serpent in the wilderness, so must the Son of Man be lifted up, that whoever believes in him may have eternal life" (3:14-15). In what must have been one of the early hymns of the church before it came to be quoted in the Letter to the Philippians, believers sang of Jesus:

> Though he was in the form of God,
>   [he] did not regard equality with God
>   as something to be exploited,
> but emptied himself,
>   taking the form of a slave,
>   being born in human likeness.
> And being found in human form,
>   he humbled himself
>   and became obedient to the point of death—
>   even death on a cross.
>
> Therefore God also highly exalted him
>   and gave him the name
>   that is above every name. (2:6-9)

In the sixth century Venantius Honorius Fortunatus wrote another hymn, more elaborate but quite in continuity with the biblical tradition:

> Sing, my tongue, the glorious battle,
> sing the ending of the fray;
> now above the cross, the trophy,
> sound the loud triumphant lay:
> tell how Christ, the world's Redeemer,
> as a victim won the day.
>
> Tell how, when at length the fullness
> of th'appointed time was come,
> Christ, the Word, was born of woman,
> left for us his heavenly home;
> showed us human life made perfect,
> shone as light amid the gloom.

Thus, with thirty years accomplished,
went he forth from Nazareth,
destined, dedicated, willing,
wrought his work, and met his death.
Like a lamb he humbly yielded
on the cross his dying breath.

Faithful cross, thou sign of triumph,
now for us the noblest tree,
none in foliage, none in blossom,
none in fruit thy peer may be;
symbol of the world's redemption,
for the weight that hung on thee![5]

Thus the cross proclaims both the humiliation of God through the act of taking on mortal flesh and the exaltation of God through the resurrection of the Incarnate and Crucified One. Humiliation-exaltation form one cohesive movement that helps us identify the many times in human history, before and since, that the great Creator of heaven and earth has wrought mighty deeds—often unseen even by the most devout; sometimes seen by the very perceptive, if only dimly; and occasionally recognized openly by all who will look.

The mystery of humiliation-exaltation can be understood best only in reverse. In terms of Jesus: Without the Resurrection, Good Friday commemorates simply the death of a martyr, a noble but tragic figure; and Christmas is simply the birth of this same ill-fated teacher. In the Gospels, the disciples are pictured throughout the ministry of Jesus as uncomprehending dolts. Furthermore, Jesus periodically does a good deed and then says, "But don't tell anyone about this." So true is this in Mark's Gospel that it has there been called "the messianic secret." Why would Jesus' ministry need to be so mystifying, even so secretive? Because until the end of the story—until the resurrection has occurred—any sense that can be made of it would be so partial as to be greatly diminished. It was not that the disciples of Jesus were more stupid than other human beings and therefore "just didn't get it." It was that neither they nor we can "get it" until we know how the story ends. The birth, ministry, and death of Jesus must be understood in light of the resurrection or the understanding will be greatly diminished. It is no accident that the observance of Christian time, the day and the week and the year, is grounded in and organized around the resurrection celebration.

The centrality of the resurrection for the Christian faith is the more apparent as today's biblical scholars piece together the way in which the first Christians wrestled with their understanding of who Jesus was. In the earliest documents of the New Testament (the letters of Paul), the revelation of Jesus as the promised Messiah of God is intimately bound up with the death and exaltation of Jesus. Paul's writings take no note of Jesus' baptism; Jesus' birth is mentioned merely in passing ("born of a woman," Gal. 4:4), in a discussion not about Jesus' incarnate relationship to us but about our relationship to God as adopted children and heirs. Yet Paul writes repeatedly about the crucifixion and resurrection of Jesus.

By the time of the writing of Mark's Gospel somewhat later, the understanding of Jesus also has to do with baptism in the Jordan, by which Jesus is identified as the one beloved by God. Matthew and Luke push the identifying events back farther: The nativity of Jesus is important if we are to understand the full story. In John, the last of the Gospels to be written (and in some of the later epistles such as Colossians), Christ has a preexistent reality, having been with God not only before the incarnation but even before creation.

Thus we have the tracks of a development across time as Christians seek more and more to make sense of what has happened in their midst. That understanding develops in gradual and sometimes tortured ways; witness the church councils that in the first three centuries formulated orthodox teachings about Christ and the Trinity. But never does the church allow to be eclipsed as its central affirmation the conviction that "the Lord is risen and at work among us."

Anamnesis and Prolepsis

The work of the Risen One, according to this conviction, occurs in the present. We asserted earlier that the present is but the thin moving edge separating past from future. But recall the "cruciform posture" of the faithful in which, fully grounded in the present, we reach out with one hand to grasp the past, and with the other the future. To state it differently, both the past and the future are in some sense brought into our present experience, particularly when we are at worship.

Anamnesis: Bringing the Past into the Present

The past becomes present by an active kind of remembrance. Usually when scripture uses the terms "remember" and "remembrance" with respect to worship it does not imply a mental process but a ritual process. At the Eucharist, we remember Jesus not by quietly thinking about him but by doing what he did: Taking bread and the cup; giving thanks over them; breaking the bread; giving the bread and cup to those who seek to be Christian disciples. This remembrance by doing rather than by cogitation falls under the Greek term *anamnesis*. Compare *amnesia*. *Amnesia* is the loss of memory. *Anamnesis* is literally "the drawing near of memory," the entrance into our own experience of that which otherwise would be locked in the past.

Thus the liturgical observance of past events somehow brings them into our own time. If this seems to be an alien concept, a brief survey of our seasonal hymnody will reveal how familiar (if unrecognized) it actually is to us. Consider the startling abundance of present-tense verbs used for past events in our hymns for Christmas, Holy Week, and Easter.

What child is this who, laid to rest, on Mary's lap *is sleeping?*
Good Christian friends, rejoice. . . . Jesus Christ *is born* today.
He *is born*, the holy child, *play* the oboe and bagpipes merrily.
O little town of Bethlehem, how still we see thee *lie.*
Come and behold him, born the King of angels.
Silent night, holy night, all *is* calm, all *is* bright.
Hark! the herald angels *sing.*

Go to dark Gethsemane. . . . Your redeemer's conflict *see; watch* with him. . . .
See, from his head, his hands, his feet, sorrow and love *flow* mingled down.
'Tis finished! The Messiah *dies, cut* off for sins, but not his own.

29

The three sad days have quickly sped; he *rises* glorious from the dead.
    Lo! Jesus *meets* thee, risen from the tomb; lovingly he *greets* thee. . .
    Hail the day that *sees* him *rise.* . . . *Reascends* his native heaven.

Note also how many of these hymn texts address the worshipers, exhorting us to take part in the past experience made present. Add to this the significant number of times our hymns use the words "now," "today," and related terms for events of the past:

    Ye who sang creation's story *now* proclaim Messiah's birth.
    This child *now* weak in infancy, our confidence and joy shall be.
    Ox and ass before him bow, and he is in the manger *now.* Christ is born *today.*
    The hopes and fears of all the years are met in thee *tonight.*

    O sacred head, *now* wounded. . . .
    This is the earth's darkest hour, but thou dost life and light restore.

    Rise from the grave *now,* O Lord, the author of life and creation.
    Christ the Lord is risen *today.*
    Now let the heavens be joyful. Let earth the song begin.

At times a hymn text is so specific about anamnesis that to sing it on any other occasion except the one it commemorates is to destroy the force of the words. Only on Christmas Eve or morning does this stanza do its fully effective work:

        Yea, Lord, we greet thee, born this happy morning,
        Jesus, to thee be all glory given.
        Word of the Father, now in flesh appearing:
        O come, let us adore him.

So intertwined are the past and the present in our experience of worship that we may not recognize the coexistence. Read slowly the following hymn texts and see if anything about them strikes you as odd.

Away in a manger, no crib for a bed,
the little Lord Jesus laid down his sweet head.
The stars in the sky looked down where he lay,
the little Lord Jesus, asleep on the hay.
The cattle are lowing, the baby awakes,
but little Lord Jesus, no crying he makes.

Low in the grave he lay, Jesus my Savior,
waiting the coming day, Jesus my Lord.
    Up from the grave he arose. . . .

Vainly they watch his bed, Jesus my Savior,
vainly they seal the dead, Jesus my Lord.

Death cannot keep its prey, Jesus my Savior.
he tore the bars away, Jesus my Lord.

If nothing strikes you as odd, probably that indicates an already high level of comfort with the interpenetration of past and present in worship. For the first four lines of "Away in a Manger" are locked in the past, in the Bethlehem of long ago. Then suddenly the verb tense shifts to the present, and we are there at Bethlehem beholding the child.

The vacillation of tenses in the Easter hymn is astonishing: "He lay, he arose" (past tense). "Vainly they watch, vainly they seal" (present tense). "Death cannot keep" (present). "He tore" (past). It is enough to make grammarians weep. But it is profound theology. I doubt that the author of the text knew anything about anamnesis in a formal sense. Likely he was not even aware that he could not maintain the same tense within a mere two lines. But from experience he knew how past and present merge in our worship. In a misguided attempt to be grammatically correct, at least one hymnal (which shall be nameless, except to say that it is not a denominational publication) has straightened the "faulty" text out by putting all verbs into the past tense. Such is the tug of a certain kind of rationalism that would remove all the mystery of anamnesis from liturgical experience.

Anamnesis does not mean that history is cyclical. It is not that the events we refer to in the present are happening again as we sing and pray. Rather it is that events that occurred only once nevertheless become contemporaneous with us because the Risen One holds all time in unity, and by the Holy Spirit brings all things to our remembrance in this way (see John 14:26). Elizabeth Clephane was accurate when she wrote: "Upon that cross of Jesus mine eye at times can see / the very dying form of One who suffered there for me." Jesus suffered only once upon the cross, but the reality of that agony comes into our experience repeatedly. Still more profound was the wisdom of the unknown author who asked a question and then declined to answer it: "Were you there when they crucified my Lord?" The answer is not given because apart from a theology of anamnesis it is nonsense: "I am there when they crucified my Lord." Because past and present are not sealed boxes, completed action enters into our time with the force of reality experienced by us.

Prolepsis: Bringing the Future into the Present

So also does the future come into our present in ways that seem to us even stranger. *Prolepsis* is a term formed from two Greek words meaning "to take beforehand." The usual definition, "anticipation," is adequate only if it means "to take something into our experience beforehand or ahead of the time at which it actually occurs." For our purposes, *prolepsis* is the bringing of God's future into our present. Again, this is a gift of the Holy Spirit wrought through the resurrection. For the resurrection is a proleptic event, a theme we shall shortly elaborate. But let it suffice for now to say that the resurrection is the entrance into the present of that future of God that is yet to be fully revealed.

Once more our hymnody may help us realize how comfortable we already are with this experience of the future being made present to us—even though our rational minds may reject it as "impossible," arguing forcefully that the future hasn't happened yet, so we cannot possibly experience it now. But note again the future present in words we often use. First with reference to the coming in glory of Christ: "Lo, he comes with clouds descending. . . . Every eye shall now behold him." We sing of the heavenly city, the new Jerusalem, as a present reality: "See, the streams of living waters, springing from eternal love, / well supply thy sons and daughters, and all fear of want remove." And again: "Zion hears the watchmen singing, / and

32

all her heart with joy is springing; / she wakes, she rises from her gloom; / for her Lord comes down all glorious."

Anamnesis and Prolepsis in Liturgy and Life

The great festivals of the church celebrate in our present experience what has occurred or what we resolutely believe will happen: The birth, ministry, suffering, death, and resurrection of Jesus; the reign of Christ in glory and the final sovereignty of God over all things. We keep this occasion not as busywork or (in the case of past events) out of mere reverence for our heritage. We keep these occasions in order that God may work in us through them and in our world through us. Once more, our hymn writers insist upon it: "O holy Child of Bethlehem, descend to us, we pray; / cast out our sin, and enter in, be born in us today." "Love so amazing, so divine, demands my soul, my life, my all." "Lord, by the stripes which wounded thee, / from death's dread sting thy servants free, / that we may live, and sing to thee: / Alleluia."

While the church's worship is always an offering to God, worship is also a great gift bestowed upon us by God; for liturgical anamnesis and prolepsis constitute a primary means by which we maintain contact with past and future, both so integral to our identity and sense of mission in the world as a people of the resurrection.

On the Nature of the Resurrection

So what is this resurrection? We think we know: A dead body comes back to life. Then why aren't we worshiping the son of the widows of Zarephath or Nain, or the daughter of Jairus, or Lazarus of Bethany? All of these are reported to have been raised from the dead; yet none became the center of so much as cultic veneration. That fact should push us beyond too superficial a view of the exaltation of the Crucified One by forcing us to ask: "When we speak of the resurrection of Jesus, do we somehow mean more (not less) than the resuscitation of a corpse?" In posing the question, I imply a positive answer. But now we must look in detail at what that answer is.

For too long popular Christianity has tamed the significance of the resurrection, treating it as a resuscitation, merely the extension in time of the earthly life of Jesus. It is an all too common belief that the dead body of Jesus was simply brought back to life by some miraculous action, some suspension or reversal of the laws of nature. But this is to settle for too little; if we persist in such a diminution, we shall shortly be left with nothing. For in medical centers daily, patients are brought back from the brink of death by advancing techniques of resuscitation. The time cannot be too far into the future when the process of death will be amenable to reversal not only after three days but after longer periods of time—not by virtue of some "miracle," but simply through increased understanding of the laws of nature. Indeed, already some people are anticipating this by having their bodies frozen at death in the hope of being brought back to life when medical technology makes sufficient advances to accomplish this. If the central event of our faith is simply the reviving of a corpse, what little we have now to hold on to will shortly dissipate entirely.

In the providence of God it may well be that our technology will now force us to look more deeply at the biblical understanding of resurrection—an understanding that is far more comprehensive and compelling than we have generally supposed. It is something other than, something far greater than a resuscitation such as that of the widows' sons in Zarephath and Nain, or of Jairus' daughter and Lazarus. Resuscitation has to do only with time—more days added to earthly life.

The resurrection of Jesus Christ is that unique act in which the intersection of time and eternity becomes evident. The resurrection is a means by which God reveals another dimension of existence at work in our midst. The Lord's victory over sin and death is a demonstration of the divine presence in a world we have viewed from too limited a perspective. It is God's word to us that there is more to reality than we can see through a telescope or under a microscope. Ever after the discovery of that empty tomb in Jerusalem, we are to look at reality through an entirely different kind of lens: the lens of God's extraordinarily powerful presence in the midst of sin and death.

Because of its very nature beyond our usual realm of time and the scientifically verifiable, the resurrection must ever remain mysterious at its core. We can understand around the edges, to be sure; and we are called to make every effort to do so. The assertion of mystery is not to be confused with intellectual laziness or acquiescence to superstition. But always the interior remains hidden; the presence of the holy is ever in part a mystery; otherwise it is not holy at all.[6]

Underlying all of this is the conviction that God simultaneously reveals and conceals divine truth. When there is nothing beyond our understanding, we are dealing not with God but with an idol created by our own limited imaginations. God's concealment is neither a punishment of us nor the result of some divine stinginess. It is simply a recognition of our limitations, a working out of the biblical conviction that

> my thoughts are not your thoughts,
>   nor are your ways my ways, says the LORD.
> For as the heavens are higher than the earth,
>   so are my ways higher than your ways
>   and my thoughts than your thoughts.
>
> (Isa. 55:8-9)

Thus there is no way in which the resurrection of Jesus Christ can be adequately explained or examined by our standard scientific tests.

The New Testament writers are insistent at this point. Paul, after discussing for fifty verses our participation in this resurrection, threw up his hands and exclaimed, "Lo! I tell you a mystery" (1 Cor. 15:51 RSV). The Gospel writers, particularly the two who wrote last, seem to go out of their way to get us out of the neat categories that cause us to assume we comprehend things fully.[7] Let us consider that in the time of Luke and John there may already have been competing understandings of the resurrection. One group came down on the side of the resuscitation of a corpse; but another group suggested an otherworldly kind of phenomenon—a ghost in some sense. Now look at what the writers say in response to such divided opinion.

In Luke's account (24:13-43) of the resurrection appearances, Jesus walks toward Emmaus with two followers (resuscitation?), but they do not recognize him (a ghost?). He teaches them; they invite him into their home and ask him to preside at the table (clearly resuscitation is implied). The Risen One breaks the bread and gives thanks (not the usual action of a ghost) and then mysteriously evaporates (hardly characteristic of a human body revived).

The two followers return to Jerusalem to report to the eleven and others gathered together what has happened. Suddenly, there is Jesus in their midst; so astounding is his apparent materialization out of thin air that "they were startled and terrified, and thought that they were seeing a ghost." There! Luke gets that theory out into the open. And just as quickly Luke deals with its inadequacy: "You think you are seeing a ghost?" says Jesus. "Touch me and feel my flesh and bones." And lest there be any lingering doubt, Jesus asks for something to eat and is given a piece of fish, which he consumes, just as we imagine a resuscitated corpse would do.

John's Gospel (chaps. 20 and 21) similarly jumps between the alternatives. Mary, well acquainted with Jesus, fails to recognize him either by sight or by sound, "supposing him to be the gardener." (A ghostly apparition?) Jesus speaks again and now Mary realizes who it is. (A corpse returned to life?) Apparently she reached out to touch him, as one would a human being. But he seems to prevent her from doing so.[8] That evening, the followers of Jesus are behind locked doors; suddenly Jesus appears. (Ghosts, but not revived corpses, are noted for materializing within sealed chambers.) But then Jesus shows them his hands and his side. Thomas, who is absent, takes this for hysteria. So one week later, once more Jesus appears, though the doors again are shut. As if to dispel the obvious conclusion that this is a ghost, Jesus invites Thomas to examine his apparently revived corpse.

The final chapter of John's Gospel is a later addition. But, as if to address again the debate about a revived corpse and ghost, the writer portrays Jesus standing on the beach (a human body?); yet those who have been closest to him do not recognize him (a ghost?). Jesus not only provides for them a catch of fish, but cooks breakfast. It is presumed that Jesus ate with them (though the text does not specify this), giving a Johannine parallel in Galilee to Luke's report of the physicality of the Risen One who eats fish in Jerusalem.

Why this vacillation in the Gospel accounts about the nature of the risen body of Jesus? But is it vacillation? Or is it rather an attempt to say, Granted we have to use human categories, because they are all we have. So naturally we think of "resuscitated corpse" or "ghost." But neither way of thinking can get at this new reality. The resurrection is beyond our usual categories. It is not less than the reviving of a corpse, but a great deal more. Yet we are stuck with our very human categories of either/or (either a body revived or a ghost); since we cannot reduce the mysterious to something more precise, we must keep bouncing from one category to the other and back again—precisely to remind ourselves that human words and ideas simply are insufficient to deal with what we have experienced in the presence of the Risen One among us.[9]

Only if we come to understand the resurrection as this wonderful and unfathomable mystery can we understand how it can be the center of the Christian interpretation of time and of all reality. Only so can we recover the conviction that the resurrection affects every-thing of significance, for the Risen Lord is seen to be the very center of the universe, the One in whom "all things hold together" (Col. 1:17). The resurrection was a kind of cosmic explosion that reverber-ated in all directions. It gave the followers of Jesus a new under-standing of the present, but also of the past and of the future. Through the resurrection (and that alone) the cross, that instrument of capital punishment by the hated Romans, ceased to be an enig-matic embarrassment and became the central symbol of the faith.

If the point had been missed before, now it was wholly evident: Eternity intersects time and in the process all prosaic understandings of temporality give way to a view of time as a vessel of divine grace, an arena of divine transformation. For the resurrection of Jesus is not primarily about some change in Jesus but about the change that God works in the world and wills to work in us. If we understand the incarnation to mean that Jesus was God in humbled action, then the exaltation of the resurrection is not some new thing that was con-ferred upon Jesus to vindicate him after his crucifixion, or to reward him for his obedience. The resurrection is restoration, not innova-tion: No glory could be given to Jesus after the incarnation that did not first belong to Christ, the Eternal Word, before the incarnation. The resurrection is not something newly added to Jesus but some-thing newly made evident to us. Before the resurrection we under-stood Jesus in human terms only; now we get at least a glimpse of that which is much grander than mortals could have imagined before or can begin to articulate with mere words.[10]

But even to say this is not to say enough; we must go even further: That which the Word of God had from the beginning and put aside

37

for three decades now is ours also; for we are to share as fully with God in the exaltation of the resurrection as God shared with us in the humiliation of the incarnation. The One who is divine partook of humanity precisely so that we who are human might partake of divinity. This "great exchange," as it has been called, may at first seem outrageous, or at least presumptuous. Can we human beings dare to hope we can be so transformed, thus to enter into the new reality we glimpse in Jesus' triumph over death? It is a matter we shall consider more fully in chapter 5. Let the testimony of the church answer the question. The traditional collect for the season of Christmas makes the point:

> O God, who wonderfully created, and yet more wonderfully restored, the dignity of human nature: Grant that we may share the divine life of him who humbled himself to share our humanity, your Son Jesus Christ; who lives and reigns with you, in the unity of the Holy Spirit, one God, for ever and ever.[11]

The prayer takes its cue from the New Testament itself, where the author of 2 Peter speaks of God's "precious and very great promises, so that through them you may . . . become participants of the divine nature" (2 Pet. 1:4).[12]

The intersection of time and eternity offers to us, the creatures of time who dwell on this planet for only a few decades, the richness of eternal grace. In the cosmic newness revealed in the resurrection of Jesus Christ we find the promise and foretaste of our own transformation. We are privileged to be participants of the divine nature. Therefore the church celebrates the resurrection of Christ and of the whole creation as the center of a weekly cycle, every Lord's day, and as the center of an annual cycle, every Easter. This the church does and will ever do, year in and year out, until time shall cease to be.

2

The Year of Our Risen Lord

The power of the resurrection, which transforms us as a body of believers, also transforms our perceptions of time—past, present, and future. For Christians, the inauguration of a new creation in Christ has produced a new organizing principle for the calendar. In some ancient cultures, including Judaism, years were counted from the date regarded as the creation of the world. In other cultures, including the Roman Empire, years were calculated in relation to the founding of the nation or to some significant event in its history. In Roman practice, for example, ancient events were counted backward from before the founding of the city, and more recent events were counted forward from the establishment of Rome. Eventually Christians combined these customs. So powerful was the revelation of God in Christ that it came to be viewed as the new creation, the event from which all else should be dated. Thereby history was divided into two parts, which English-speaking Christians have customarily designated B.C. and A.D.[1] But that is to get ahead of the story, for this division of years did not occur until centuries after the resurrection. What occurred at once was a new designation within the week.

Sunday: The Lord's Day,
the First and the Eighth Day

The seven-day week was the ancient heritage of several Mideastern cultures. Among the Jews, the final day of this week was set aside as an occasion for the adoration of God and for the commemoration of divine acts of grace, which occasion such worship. This day was called "the sabbath," meaning simply "the seventh."[2] It came to commemorate the seventh day of creation as reported in Genesis 2:2.[3] A code of regulations arose to ensure its proper observance among the devout.

Christians saw in the resurrection profound evidence of the renewal of the first creation, which had become ruined by human rebellion and thus was alienated from the Creator. Easter was the inauguration of a new era, the new creation in Christ (2 Cor. 5:17; Gal. 6:15). None other than the Creator had redeemed the world from its sin by a stunning act of self-sacrifice and reversal. Therefore, in addition to going to the synagogue on the seventh day, the early Christians assembled to rejoice in the resurrection on the first day of the week, as reported in Acts 20:7 and 1 Corinthians 16:2.

This first day of the week is "the Lord's Day"—that is, the day Christ has claimed and hallowed by escaping from the dominion of death. There is an important ambiguity in the term; for "the Lord's Day" is intentionally related to a phrase used by the Hebrew prophets and again in the New Testament, "the day of the Lord."[4] This latter phrase implies the judgment and reign of God's righteousness at the end of time. So the weekly observance of the Lord's Day announces that the just and unending dominion of God has already begun in the coming of Christ.

Here, then, is an example of the model of time proposed in chapter 1, in which the present is that thin, ever-moving edge between the past and the future: On any given Lord's Day, the worshiping church in the present fleeting moment grasps both the past (by commemorating through *anamnesis* the Lord's resurrection and all that served to prepare for it) and the future (by affirming through *prolepsis* the fulfilled reign of God, the Day of the Lord). Both of these are made present to us as we experience the transforming power of the resurrection in our lives and thereby begin to live even now in the ways of the future. All of time is thus bound together in the day of worship itself.

But a second title is given to the first day of the week; in words that are at first puzzling and then engaging, Sunday is called "the eighth day." This term was much loved by the writers of the second and third centuries, who insisted that the church is now in the eighth day of creation. In the symbolism of numbers, seven was a number signifying completion. But eight, extending beyond seven, was a number of redemption. What is implicit in 1 Peter 3:20 concerning the symbolic significance of number eight ("Eight persons were saved through water" in Noah's ark) quickly becomes explicit in early Christian writing. In the second-century epistle of *Barnabas*, we read words attributed to God: "When resting from all things, I shall begin the eighth day, that is, the beginning of the other world"; then the author comments to the reader concerning early liturgical practice: "For this reason we observe the eighth day with gladness, in which Jesus rose from the dead and, having manifested himself to his disciples, ascended into heaven" (*Barn.* 13:9-10). This then was the early way of counting: In six days God created the physical world, and on the seventh day rested; but in the humiliation-exaltation of Jesus, God inaugurated the new creation in Christ, thus constituting the eighth day of creation.[5]

But there is a difficulty here. The week has only seven days. Hence the first day of the week and the eighth day of the week are the same day. Yet even in that there is meaning: The creation of the cosmos (which God began on Day One) and the new creation are not antagonistic to each other; we do not have to leave the physical world in order to participate in the new creation in Christ, even though this second creation ultimately will endure beyond the decay of the first creation. There is in Western music an interesting if accidental analogy that clarifies this idea. In the standard musical scale, the first note and the eighth note ("the octave") are the same—and yet different. The two notes cohere totally in ways that no other tones of the eight-note series do, yet they are not identical. So Sunday is both the first and the eighth day of the week in complementary relationship. As the eighth note of the scale is consonant with but higher than the first, so the new creation does not demean the creation of the cosmos, but reveals to us fuller insights into the Creator's purpose and providence.[6]

The church's first and eighth day recalls not only the formation of the universe and the inauguration of the reign of God in Christ in the resurrection; it also commemorates the instituting of the church by the Holy Spirit on the Day of Pentecost on the first day of the week (Acts 2). The writer of a hymn text, using the metaphor of light, addresses Sunday (the "thee" of the stanza) in this way:

> On thee, at the creation, the light first had its birth;
> on thee, for our salvation, Christ rose from depths of earth;
> on thee, our Lord, victorious, the Spirit sent from heaven;
> and thus on thee, most glorious, a triple light was given.[7]

The notion of light has itself been important to the interpretation of the Lord's Day. Set in the midst of a culture that named the weekdays after deities, Christians were confronted with a potentially embarrassing situation: The day for their exaltation of Christ risen from the dead was, in the world around them, the day dedicated to the sun god. How was the church to dispel the notion that it was simply doing obeisance to the solar deity on the sun's day? Theological inventiveness soon took hold as people remembered a verse from Malachi: "The sun of justice will rise with healing in its (or, his) wings" (Mal. 4:2).[8] This passage made two points of connection at once: (1) Christ is the true light of the world; who made and far outshines the sun in glory. The brightness of Christ is not merely physical radiance but justice, which saves the world from the evil and injustice that continually afflict it. (2) The rising (understood as rising from the dead) of this Sun of Justice is central to salvation. Thus the church turned to its great benefit the potentially embarrassing fact that the Risen Christ is worshiped on the day dedicated to a nature deity in other religious systems of that time. Those nature religions now could be seen as incomplete strivings after the truth made known fully in Christ. The "sun's day" was, in fact, the "Sun's day"; since the Great Sun is Christ, the Lord's Day could, without need for apology, be properly called "Sunday."

Indeed, the idea of Christ as the Great Sun accorded well with a passage in the Revelation, in which the writer reports of the heavenly Jerusalem in the new creation: "The city has no need of sun or moon to shine on it, for the glory of God is its light, and its lamp is the Lamb" (Rev. 21:23). This amplified another central meaning of the Lord's Day: That it is a foretaste of heaven, an anticipation of the joy of eternity. As the saints above praise God perpetually, so the saints below join them in corporate praise at least once each week. The Lord's Day thus points to, promises, and proclaims the Day of the Lord.

The weekly observance of Sunday as a longing for and a prefiguring of the eternal justice of God has been eclipsed in recent decades, probably because yearning for God's reign was judged to be a neurotic (or at least an inappropriate) escape from present responsibility. But having fled one potentially serious danger, we have run headlong into another, worse predicament. A present that

42

has no hope for the future is full of bleakness; for every present age is replete with injustice and misery that seem the more irremediable apart from confidence that God will overcome all wrong. The resurrection of Jesus in itself arouses that confidence within us and points us to the Great Sunday, the final Day of the Lord's salvation foretold by the prophets of Israel.

One indication that this future aspect of Sunday has not been completely lost in our time is found in Duke Ellington's text "Come Sunday." At the beginning of this hymn it is easy to suppose that the singer is only looking forward to the next Sunday in the secular calendar: "Come Sunday, oh, come Sunday, that's the day." But upon reading further we meet this:

> Heaven is a goodness time,
> a brighter light on high.
> "Do unto others as you would have them do unto you,"
> and have a brighter by and by.
>
> I believe God is now,
> was then, and always will be.
> With God's blessing we can
> make it through eternity.[9]

Profound theology characterizes this seemingly simple set of words. Here Sunday, the first day of our calendar week, is a metaphor for and intimation of eternal life. The singer prays not for the coming of the day after Saturday but for nothing less than the full reign of God. Note also the fusion of past, present, and future. In the opening stanza Ellington puts us in touch with the past by recounting the first creation: "I believe that God put sun and moon up in the sky." The citation of the words of Jesus, commonly called the Golden Rule, brings into consciousness our present task; for we seek to walk now in the ways that characterize the final triumph of God. And we pray for the great, eternal Sunday when, with all of the hosts of heaven, we praise God and the Lamb without ceasing. For the Christian, all of time is a seamless whole.

The regularity of Sundays on earth is crucial to all we are setting forth here. Once every seven days a holy day is kept, rain or shine, summer and winter, whether parishioners attend or go instead to the mountains, the beach, the corner hangout, or stay at home in bed. Sunday occurs once each week. Not only can we not prevent this, but we insist on marking it with worship. This is not insignificant, nor is it simply an old habit the institutional church has not yet managed to shake. Rather it is an affirmation of the continuing and dependable presence and activity of God in creation, even when that creation is indifferent to (or even disdainful of) divine goodness.

In some religious systems adherents come together only on infrequent and widely separated holy days; at other times persons may come to a priest or religious teacher for individual counsel, but regular corporate worship is not the rule. But among those three intertwined religions that grew up in the Middle East, worship once every seven days in synagogues, churches, and mosques is not an option but a necessity. Amid human distractions and idolatries, the faithfulness of God must be proclaimed in the congregation with regularity. Spasmodic worship could seem to connote a deity who appears in our lives only sporadically or whose help is needed only when we are in crisis; but a God who works continually in our midst, even when we are indifferent or oblivious to that work, calls forth worship frequently and systematically.

That is why for Christians Sunday is the chief festival occasion of the faith. About this there is much misunderstanding. Many active Christians would say that Christmas is their chief festival. Closer to the mark, but still missing it, are those who would say that Easter Day is the principal feast of the church. What is amiss about such assessments? Simply this: No observance that occurs only once a year can connote the continuing work of God in daily life. Therefore the chief festival occurs weekly, and from it all else is derived, including those annual festivities that may be more visible and certainly are the more popular cultural occasions.[10]

The Lord's Day and the Week

From the First Day of the week, the meaning of the rest of the week is derived. The congregation that worships together on the Lord's Day continues its worship throughout the week, though necessarily in a dispersed manner. In the contemporary world, work schedules and distances from the seat of the Sunday assembly preclude daily services of worship Mondays through Saturdays that compare in size with those on Sunday. But two things need to be noted well.

First, historically the church has had brief weekday services known as "the daily office."[11] In its older and simpler form, these services were conducted each day only in the principal church of the area, the cathedral. Townspeople on their way to or from work could attend, and hence this "cathedral office" was observed twice daily: morning prayer (or matins) and evening prayer (or evensong, if primarily sung rather than spoken). A more complex regimen arose in monastic communities, which developed a system of seven or eight offices to be said daily. Even to our day, morning and evening daily services are scheduled in some places (usually cathedral churches). Though only a limited number of communities of believers could hold such services, and though only a portion within that community could attend with regularity, the very existence of such a program of daily worship is a reminder to all of the importance of regular prayer. The continuing existence of the fuller regimen of daily prayer within monastic houses is a reminder to all Christians of the call to "pray without ceasing" (1 Thess. 5:17) and also an action done on behalf of the whole church. Those in such monastic communities see their prayer not primarily as private devotional duty to God but as an offering made in the name and on behalf of all those Christians who cannot devote themselves so singularly to a daily schedule of services.

Second, those who cannot attend the daily services are nevertheless to engage in prayer wherever they are; and while so engaged they (like the monastics) pray not as isolated individuals but as members of the community of faith, separated in space but united in Christ. It should be a great encouragement to Christians to know that at every hour of the day and night, somewhere in the world prayer is being offered up both by communities of Christians (whether in religious orders or in local congregations) and by individuals. Never is the church without articulated prayer. How perceptive was the writer of an evening hymn who praises God, as our day of prayer comes to a close and we prepare to sleep:

> We thank thee that thy church, unsleeping
> while earth rolls onward into light,

> through all the world her watch is keeping,
> and rests not now by day or night.
>
> As o'er each continent and island
> the dawn leads on another day,
> the voice of prayer is never silent,
> nor die the strains of praise away.[12]

In some communities of prayer, specific days of the week took on special meaning. Friday and Saturday, in particular, were given emphasis. Since Friday was the day of Jesus' death, it was the weekly approach to the Lord's Day of resurrection. Fasting was appropriate, even if only in the substitution of fish for meat to remind the believer that the flesh of Jesus hung upon the cross; Saturday, the day in the sepulchre, was a day of quiet spiritual preparation for the Sunday feast. Wednesday often was set aside as a kind of midpoint, lest the busyness of Monday through Friday cause Christians to forget that every day is a day of prayer. But whether certain weekdays are given particular meaning or not, the weekly observance of the resurrection is intended to hallow all of the days that follow the First Day. Sunday sets the stage for all else. This is quite contrary to our cultural practices. We have been acculturated to regard Sunday as the last day of the weekend, not the first day of the week. In the working world, Monday is the first day of the week, unless the weekend is extended by a Monday holiday. If the whole week is to be hallowed by the humiliation-exaltation of God in Christ, we need a reorientation of our thinking.

Can the church again see Sunday as the First Day, as the Lord's Day, as the Eighth Day? Reorientation may well begin by changing our language. Despite the clever theological twist given to "Sunday" by exalting Christ as the risen Sun of Justice, that designation will always say less to us than "Lord's Day," "First Day," or "Eighth Day." Calvinists, in particular, are to be thanked for retaining the use of the first phrase and members of The Society of Friends for preserving the second. Despite that, neither term is widely used within the church or even recognized by many who attend with regularity. Send invitations to friends who are practicing Christians to come to dinner at your home on "next Lord's Day" or even "next First Day," and then brace yourself for the spate of phone calls asking for clarification of the date. (Don't even bother to invite them to

46

arrive on the "next Eighth Day.") The reintroduction of these terms into the working vocabulary of Christians could do much to heighten our awareness of ancient and enduringly crucial faith statements.

Today's church needs to wrestle with deeds as well as words, however. Since the Lord's Day connotes a uniquely central act of God, how can God's people make this day distinctive in relation to the rest of the week? The Lord's Day is not primarily a day for abstaining from certain kinds of activities for the sake of abstinence itself; nor is it primarily a day off work. Until the time of Constantine, in fact, Sunday only rarely coincided with the holidays of the Greco-Roman world (which did not adhere to a seven-day week). Christians were constrained to put in a full day's work and yet worship their Lord either well into the night (the vigil service), or very early in the morning. In later Christian practice some groups, such as the English Puritans, sternly forbade all possible forms of "nonreligious" activity on the Lord's Day. Food to be eaten on that day had to be prepared on Saturday. Religious literature could be read on Sunday; secular material could not. Even ordinarily accepted games and sporting activities were banned. The result, achieved in a misguided imitation of Hebraic sabbath ("rest") rules, often was an oppressive legalism that made the First Day a time to be dreaded rather than anticipated with joy.

Now we are at the other end of the spectrum. If Sunday is not dreaded, neither is it anticipated with great joy; for often it is simply like any other day, or at least little different from Saturday. The suppression of so-called Sunday blue laws has a sound basis in civil law, particularly in nations that cherish the separation of church and state and have within them a variety of religious groups that observe different weekly holy days. But perhaps it is time for Christians (as a matter of discipline and piety, not of devising and imposing a legal code), to consider seriously how we ourselves can distinguish the First Day. Can it become once again a time of refreshment to invigorate us for ministry during the rest of the week rather than being simply a continuation of the usual rat race, or the last weekend day during which we must brace ourselves for the hectic workweek about to begin?

For many people, Sunday evening is necessarily a time to begin the new workweek: to make the lesson plans or to do the homework put off until the last minute, to do the laundry similarly deferred, to review the week's agenda, to fly to another city for a meeting that starts Monday morning. For the devout, Sunday morning schedules conspire to make that time as spiritually distracting as Sunday evening can be; in most households people are so busy getting organized to get to church on time that they are unable to deal with anything else on Sunday morning. So how is the Lord's Day to be kept effectively in such an environment? Allow a modest if unusual proposal that may be the start of a way out of this morass.

Suppose that mentally we shift the way we calculate time, at least on the weekends, and recover our Hebraic heritage of reckoning days from sunset to sunset. Mentally ending the Lord's Day at sunset on Sunday allows for the necessary Sunday evening tasks to be done as a part of the work of the second day of the Christian week. But more important, to discipline ourselves to regard the Lord's Day as beginning on Saturday evening allows time for spiritual preparation that cannot be squeezed into the schedules of most church-going families the next morning.[13] Such a reordering of Christian thinking, contrary as it is to prevailing cultural customs, could be the beginning of a new way of seeing the whole of Christian faith as a reinterpretation of commonly accepted ideas and values.

There may be other and better ways to achieve this goal; but any system of Christian thought that does not reinterpret and indeed overthrow prevailing ideas and values has not grasped the drastic implications of the resurrection of Jesus Christ; nor does it reckon with the reaction to the first Christians by others in their culture: "These people who have been turning the world upside down have come here also" (Acts 17:6). The church by nature is always something of a counterculture organization; sensing this, the dominant cultures ever will seek to domesticate that church. When they succeed too well (as often they have done), the gospel entrusted to the church may be severely compromised. Then the church, to survive with integrity, must enter into an era of self-examination and reformation. We seem to be in need of just such an era.

48

The Lord's Day and the Year of the Lord

As the First Day begins and sanctifies the week, so also the Lord's Day has priority over and determines the calendar called the liturgical year. We have already noted how contrary this is to prevailing assumptions. It is usually taken for granted that because of the appeal of their liturgical celebrations and due to the general popularity of customs surrounding their observance, Christmas and Easter are the primary feasts of the church. But, in fact, the primary Christian feast must occur weekly, not annually, in order to testify to the way in which the humiliation-exaltation of God in Christ has transformed the totality of human life. On the basis of this assertion, the otherwise apparently strange organization of the remainder of this book may begin to make sense.

The weekly feast of the church takes precedence over any annual festival. It follows that the yearly festival of first rank should be that which most closely in tone reflects the weekly observance. Therefore, of the annual observances of the church, Easter has preeminence. (This, again, is countercultural for most of us, since the mercantile world has exalted Christmas over Easter because of its greater commercial potential, arising from the exchange of gifts and greeting cards and from the popularity of social functions with their attendant concerns for food, entertainment, and decorating.) "Easter" here means not simply Easter Day but the entire season that day inaugurates. Since this season embraces fifty days, its concluding occasion, the Day of Pentecost, is thereby assigned its due place in the ordering of yearly celebrations.

Lent, a preparation for the annual resurrection observance, naturally is derived from Easter and secondary to it. This is not always evident in practice. In many Protestant recoveries of the liturgical calendar, until recently Lent was observed as a forty-six-day season of great spiritual emphasis and sometimes frenetic parish activity, while Easter was kept only as a day, not as the Great Fifty Days; this gave the very misleading impression that Lent is more important than Easter. Such a misunderstanding needs to be corrected aggressively.

Easter preceded by Lent is the primary annual cycle of the calendar; secondary to it is Christmas preceded by Advent. This is true both theologically and historically. It is the resurrection that interprets the birth of Jesus. Apart from the resurrection, Jesus has no more claim upon us than Socrates, Abraham Lincoln, Mohandas Gandhi, Martin Luther King, Jr., or Anwar Sadat: He was simply one among many good leaders who managed to meet an unjust death. This theological assertion is buttressed by historical facts: (1) What is presumably the oldest of the four Gospels pays no attention whatever to the birth of Jesus, beginning instead with the account of his baptism; and Paul makes only passing references to Jesus' birth (as in Galatians 4:4 and Philippians 2:7). Only later did Matthew and Luke attach enough importance to the nativity to comment upon it extensively. (2) Even more significant: Although the resurrection was observed liturgically in the church from its very inception, the earliest recorded liturgical observance of Christmas Day falls well into the fourth century.

In light of all this, we will discuss the Advent-Christmas cycle (chaps. 5 and 6) only after covering the Lent-Easter cycle (chaps. 3 and 4). Taken together, these observances cover almost exactly one-half of the solar year; they are balanced by a second half (called by the often misunderstood term "Ordinary Time"), set forth in chapter 7. There is then a separate cycle of observances that range over the full solar year and that celebrate the transforming activity of God in the lives of particular individuals who are commonly called "saints" (though we shall have to define that term carefully). This "sanctoral cycle" is in turn subservient to everything that precedes it and hence falls in chapter 8.

It must be admitted that this is not the way books on the Christian calendar are usually constructed. For reasons to be discussed in subsequent chapters, usually such a book begins with the fourth Sunday prior to Christmas Day and works its way in order through the next fifty-two weeks. But such linear interpretations of the calendar often obscure the theological relationships within that calendar; hence, a very different pattern of organization is used here, not for the sake of novelty but out of theological desirability.

Relationship of Calendar and Lectionary

Those who do not use a lectionary (any lectionary) and do not intend to do so, can find much applicable material in succeeding chapters, assuming they do wish to observe traditional liturgical occasions in some fashion. But these readers are excused from looking at this section and may now go directly to chapter 3. Those who do use a lectionary (and particularly the currently popular three-year one) may wish to continue reading here, and thus to consider pertinent issues of cause and effect.

Anyone who was active before 1970 in churches that observe a calendar can recognize vast changes that have occurred since then. The extent of the changes varies from one denomination to another; but the fact of alteration is universal. Nor is it an accident that for the 1970 liturgical year, a new lectionary was put in place by Roman Catholics. This system of scripture readings for public worship was then altered in relatively slight ways and adopted in varying forms by many Protestants. The question thus arises: Did readings chosen for the new lectionary create a different understanding of the meaning of observances such as Lent; or did altered understandings of the meaning of liturgical time such as Lent dictate which readings would be chosen for the revised lectionary? The only satisfactory answer is "Both."

This is not quite the old "chicken-egg problem," in which one thing presumably must have preceded the other. Rather, here we have a dynamic interaction of factors across time. Because Lent was seen as a season preliminary to Easter, in some older interpretations Lent was predominantly or even exclusively about the suffering and death of Jesus. (Until the recent wave of hymnal revisions, typically in Protestant hymnals the section labeled "Lent" contained nothing except hymns about the events of Holy Week, which thereby got extended backward to Ash Wednesday.) Lent was the season of the cross. Period.

But those serious about the pursuit of Christian history had to wrestle with the fact that Lent began as a time of final instruction and intensive preparation for baptism. Ancient lectionaries (or at least portions of them) were reconstructed and found to contain Lenten readings such as the story of the man born blind (John 9); for in the early centuries baptism was likened to the recovery of sight. Hence in 1970 John 9:1-41 became the Gospel for the Fourth Sunday in Lent of Year A. This lectionary inclusion, grounded in a very old understanding of Lent as preparation for baptism, helped to reestab-

51

lish Lent in the church as a season for the consideration of the meaning of baptism as related to the new life we have in Christ, the Crucified and Risen One. Thus the meaning of a season dictated the choice of new readings, which in turn dictated a reconsideration of how the season is to be observed. This is what I mean by a dynamic interaction that goes beyond the simplicity of a "chicken-egg" question.

It is beyond the scope of this book to comment on the way in which a day's readings determine or interpret the meaning of each calendar occasion, though specific Sundays within the Lent-Easter and Advent-Christmas cycles will be discussed; but those who use the lectionary are encouraged to look for such connections week by week and to make good use of them through preaching and other media to set forth in the congregation a renewed understanding of liturgical time.

3

Easter: The Great Fifty Days

"Easter" is an ambiguous and unfortunate term. The ambiguity resides in its double meaning: (1) the period of eight Sundays, comprising fifty days, often called as a unit "the Great Fifty Days"; (2) the opening day of this period, better called "Easter Day" than "Easter," in order to distinguish it from the first meaning. The second meaning is what comes into the minds of most people when they hear the term "Easter," but the first meaning is more ample and accurate, and the one that Christian people need to be taught to embrace. For the explosive force of the resurrection of the Lord is too vast to be contained within a celebration of one day. "Easter" is an unfortunate term because apart from popular associations, it has no obvious Christian meaning, but may be a variation of "Œstre" or "Eastre," a Teutonic goddess of springtime and hence of fertility. The word may relate well to those secondary indicators of the season: sunrise, eggs (obvious signs of fertility), and—in the north temperate zone—the tulips, daffodils, and hyacinths of early spring.[1] But "Easter" as a name fails to say anything about Jesus Christ and is possibly a remnant of a polytheistic nature cult. The best to be said (and this is an obvious rationalization) is that by the power of the resurrection Christ has fulfilled and displaced the longing for the life that the goddess of springtime once represented.

The more venerable term for the resurrection observance is "Pasch," from the Greek word we translate as "Passover."[2] While "Pasch" may at first seem odd and esoteric, the English-speaking church would do well to recover it, and indeed already knows it in its adjectival form. Paul refers to Christ as our "paschal lamb" (1 Cor. 5:7 RSV and NRSV), and a number of hymns use the term "Paschal," particularly those for Easter Day and the Eucharist.[3] Among the languages of Western Europe, English and German are unusual in not preserving some form of "Pasch" as their preferred title for the resurrection observance. In the other tongues we find: *pasques*,

53

Italian; *pâques*, French; *paaske*, Danish; *paasch*, Dutch; *pasg*, Welsh; and *pascua*, Spanish. While English-speaking Christians will never abandon the term "Easter," the increased use of "Pasch" and "Paschal" needs to be encouraged, not only to put us in line with related language systems but to assert the unique Christian meaning of the observance.

The use of "Pasch" first emphasizes the continuity between the Hebraic and Christian traditions; although for complex historical reasons the dates of the Jewish Passover and the Christian Passover never exactly coincide, and in some years are separated by weeks, nevertheless as Christians we affirm that the resurrection of our Lord is related intimately to the exodus from Egypt.[4] The crucifixion of Jesus took place during the Passover season, and this link is maintained in the annual observances of the two events. There is a historic affinity between the living faith of Judaism and the holiest Christian season that does not exist between that season and the rites of a forgotten Teutonic goddess.

Of greater importance is the meaning of that affinity. Christianity not only grew out of Judaism but, until the rise of anti-Semitism, saw itself as the natural outgrowth and culmination of Judaism, not as its radical rejection and violent overthrow. The first Christians (all of them Jews) inescapably saw a symbolic continuity between the slaughtered lamb of the Passover Seder and the crucified Lamb of God. Further, as Moses led the Israelites through the sea into freedom from bondage to Pharaoh, so Jesus Christ through the resurrection provides "the way out" (the literal meaning of "exodus") of bondage to sin and death. To speak of Christ as "our Pasch" or "our Passover" can be an affirmation that Christianity is a development out of Judaism, not a drastic displacement of the Hebraic faith.[5]

The annual Paschal observance is closely connected to the weekly observance of the Lord's Day. It has become a maxim of late that "every Sunday is a little Easter." But it would be more accurate to say that "every Easter is a great Sunday." In the foregoing chapter we established the priority of Sunday in the Christian calendar. To say that "every Sunday is a little Easter" seems to transfer that priority from the weekly to the annual observance. Further, if not interpreted with great care, the popular saying can be taken to mean that the weekly service must strive to be an Easter celebration in miniature. Granted, every Lord's Day the church proclaims the life, death, resurrection, and reign of the One who is its head; but if every Sunday is to be a mini-Easter there may be a great deal of frustration in the planning of local weekly worship and even a diminished role for the annual observance. Consider then that "every Easter is a great Sunday," a time, in effect, to reflect more deeply and with a greater degree of sustained concentration upon what the church affirms weekly about the work of God in our midst. Easter, in effect, puts Sunday under the magnifying glass—but only when Easter itself is seen as a season, not simply as a single day.

Easter Season: The Week of Weeks

That Easter in its fullness consists of fifty days is no accident. For it is based on the great Jewish festival of fifty days that began with the opening of the harvest season two days after the start of Passover and extended until what came to be called the Day of Pentecost.[6] Here again the theological symbolism of numbers becomes significant.

The number seven was highly revered among the Jews. Among other meanings, seven connoted fullness: On the seventh day of creation God celebrated the fullness of all created things. The number came to be enshrined in the time period known as a week.[7] But if seven was a good number, how much better must be forty-nine (seven squared). So a forty-nine-day period was a "week of weeks": As one-seventh of the week is set aside as holy, so also one-seventh of the year (or as close as we can come to it in even weeks) is held in special regard.

Fifty also came to be a number of sacred meaning. Recall the legislation in Leviticus 25 about the Year of Jubilee, said to occur every fiftieth year. So radical is this code that scholars suggest it could never have actually been observed but was only an ideal to be sought. However that may be, the overthrow of business as usual during the Year of Jubilee reveals the eschatological character of "fifty"—it is a number of liberation and restitution, an occasion for great joy. So it is not illogical that the spring harvest festival of the forty-nine days was closed by a fiftieth day as a sign of newness and rejoicing. The church readily adapted this symbolism for its own purposes. Christ is fullness heaped upon fullness (cf. John 1:16), and so can be symbolized by seven times seven. The resurrection itself is the Great Fiftieth Day, even as it is the Eighth Day of the week: an entrance into a new kind of existence, a way of sharing even now in that which is yet to come. As Israel rejoiced in the spring harvest for fifty days, beginning two days after Passover, so the church rejoiced in the resurrection for fifty days, starting two days after the offering up of Christ, the Paschal Lamb, upon the cross. It was all perfect, both in its symmetry and in the logic of its symbolism.

The recovery of Easter as "the Great Fifty Days" of the year can move the church along toward a fuller understanding of what the resurrection of its Lord implies. Easter is not one closing day at the end of a lengthy period of Lent. Easter is one extended rejoicing in the resurrection that more than exceeds in length the Lenten disciplines. The first day of the season, Easter Day, is the opening of a protracted celebration, even as the Resurrection is itself the opening to a vast new reality.

The revised liturgical calendar of most denominations is helping to press this point. For centuries the church had designated one Sunday as "Easter" and called subsequent Sundays "the First [Second through Sixth] Sunday After Easter." Now the inaugural occasion of the Great Fifty Days is entitled "Easter Day," and subsequent Sundays are "the Second [Third through Seventh] Sunday of Easter." The change in terminology is not to be undervalued. "The First Sunday After Easter" implies Easter is over, having lasted only one day. But "the Second Sunday of Easter" (for the same date) indicates that Easter is an extended season, whose essential character is shared by all of its parts. The careful use of "Easter Day" rather than "Easter" for the opening occasion further presses this point.

Once Easter is seen as a season, congregations can work at distinctive worship practices throughout the Great Fifty Days in order to tie the weeks together more clearly in the hearts of worshipers. For example, on Sundays Two through Seven, one stanza of a hymn used on Easter Day might be sung as an acclamation ("Christ the Lord Is Risen Today" is a logical choice). Or a special seasonal prayer can be used on each of these Sundays. The character of the eighth Sunday, the Day of Pentecost, differs from that of the first seven and will be discussed later in this chapter. The Council of Nicea A.D. 325 high-

lighted the special character of the Great Fifty Days by ruling that
during the period two practices commonly kept during the rest of
the year were forbidden: fasting and kneeling. In our day congregations that normally kneel to receive communion might instead stand
for all receptions of the sacrament throughout the Fifty Days, and
should be helped to see this posture as an affirmation of our own
share in the resurrection: We shall be raised from death and shall
stand with Christ in glory.[8]

Congregations that do not observe the Eucharist weekly but are
intrigued by the possibility (yet fearful of instituting it all at once)
may well use Easter as a season in which to experiment with having
the Eucharist each Sunday. The joyous character of the season can
assist in moving beyond the sometimes morose associations
wrongly attached to the sacrament; and the sacrament can be seen
primarily as a feast of faith with the Risen Lord rather than as a
funereal commemorative meal eaten by the disciples of an executed
teacher.

Before proceeding it may be helpful to explain what may seem to
be the strange arrangement of the content in the sections following.
We are going to discuss first the character of the whole season of
Easter (including Ascension and the Day of Pentecost), while holding Easter Day itself in abeyance. Then we are going back to a
consideration of Easter Day, though only touching upon its Great
Vigil (which will be discussed further as the conclusion of the
Triduum in chapter 4). The reasons for what may seem like walking
backward are both theological and practical. At the theological level,
we have set forth in chapter 1 the conviction that the whole gospel
story has to be understood in reverse: Until the resurrection, even
the disciples of Jesus could make no sense of his ignominious death
at Calvary. And until the crucifixion they completely misinterpreted
what Jesus' ministry was about. Furthermore, only once the ministry, death, and resurrection got set in order did the birth of Jesus
come to take on theological importance. After that, the church had
to consider what role the incarnate Word of God had played prior
to the incarnation, in the very creation itself and before. Christian
theology inevitably has to be done in retrospect.

There are also practical considerations. The Great Vigil is the
inaugural event of Easter Day. Easter Day in its entirety is the

inaugural event of the Great Fifty Days. Inaugurations are by their very nature intended to be intimations of what lies ahead. Therefore until we consider what is to follow, we cannot rightly plan the inaugural events, for we do not know what they are to announce and encapsulate. Often inaugural events in the worship of the church suffer a kind of anemia by coming to be looked upon as culminations rather than introductions. Thus in the popular mind Easter ends on Easter Day (as Christmas ends on Christmas Day). Perhaps by "walking backward" we can discover more adequately what we are attempting to proclaim and experience in our Easter liturgies.

The Great Fifty Days: Sunday by Sunday

The opening week of Easter in the ancient church had a distinctive character. Each day those who had been initiated into the church at the Great Vigil attended worship wearing the new white robes given to them after their baptism; in the daily sermon, the preacher interpreted for them the meanings of Christian life and faith implied in the rites of initiation. Thus Augustine, Bishop of Hippo, addressed newly baptized Africans in this way during Easter Week:

> A sermon is directed to all the faithful when it advocates the ordering of [human] life and encourages the practice of virtue, so that everlasting life may be both sought and attained. But at this time we are directing our words chiefly to you, the new offshoots of grace, reborn of water and the Holy Spirit, planted and watered by our ministry in the garden of God who gives the increase.

> Regard yourselves as delivered out of Egypt from a harsh servitude, where iniquity ruled over you; and as having passed through the Red Sea by baptism, in which you received the seal of Christ's bloody cross. Prune yourselves therefore of past sins, those enemies of yours which pursued you from the rear. For as the Egyptians perished in the very waters traversed by the people of God, so your sins were blotted out in the waters in which you were baptized.[9]

Easter Week was thus a time during which converts reflected on the import of their new faith, while more mature Christians reviewed the basics and looked for deeper meanings than they had discovered before. That is a crucial clue to the observance of the entire Easter season; it is a time for both discovery and reconsideration, for a return to the basics of our faith in the Risen One in the conviction that those basics have reverberations sufficient to touch Christians from the newest to the most experienced. The season of Easter should be in every congregation a time for an unapologetic and aggressive reaffirmation of essential Christian faith.

Among those who follow one of the versions of the contemporary ecumenical lectionary, that reaffirmation is given a particular shape we will now consider bit by bit. Those who do not customarily use the lectionary will nevertheless find some of this material already in place by virtue of accepted chronologies: The Sunday following Easter Day is the time to consider the story of Thomas. The Thursday of the Sixth Week marks the fortieth day of the resurrection; thus it (or the Sunday thereafter) commemorates the ascension. The fiftieth day is Pentecost Sunday. Beyond that, even those who do not usually follow the lectionary may find its use beneficial throughout Easter, or at least may draw from it principles for organizing these weeks.

The Second Sunday of Easter: Thomas Sunday

The process of reaffirmation commended above can be given particular shape on the Second Sunday of Easter.[10] Thomas, having been absent for the appearance of the Lord in the midst of the disciples a week earlier, now is confronted by the Risen One. The story in John 20 is not primarily about the doubts Thomas has (or we have); that is to put the emphasis at the wrong place. The focus is on the graciousness of Christ in meeting our doubts. Jesus did not say about Thomas: "So he was absent when I appeared. Tough! Let him figure it out as best he can." Instead Jesus appears to Thomas and says, in effect, "Come and see, and thus believe."

Nor is there an implied criticism of Thomas in the final sentence of the story: "Blessed are those who have not seen and yet have come to believe." "Blessed" is a meager English word that seems to put the onus on us: We must do the right thing in order to be accounted acceptable. But the Greek, better translated as "happy" or "joyous," can speak more of God's grace. Happiness is a gift rather than an achievement. Thus this concluding verse is not to be taken to mean, "OK, Thomas. You had to have proof. Think how inferior you are to all of those later followers of mine who will have to believe without any proof." That is to get the story upside down. Look at it (as all of scripture should be viewed) from the standpoint of divine action rather than human reaction: "Those who cannot see me in the flesh will nevertheless be enabled by grace to believe, even as you have been, Thomas. For I, the Risen One, am gracious. By the power of my resurrection I am able to share myself as a gift with all in every age and circumstance who truly seek me." (Is not this the core meaning of the presence of the Holy Spirit in our midst? But that is to get ahead of the story.)

A venerable old hymn of many stanzas has been appropriately segmented into two divisions in some hymnals; certain stanzas, which narrate the story of Easter morning, are to be sung on Easter Day. But the following stanzas are for Thomas Sunday:

> When Thomas first the tidings heard,
> how they had seen the risen Lord,
> he doubted the disciples' word.
>
> "My pierced side, O Thomas, see;
> my hands, my feet, I show to thee;
> not faithless but believing be."
>
> No longer Thomas then denied;
> he saw the feet, the hands, the side;
> "Thou art my Lord and God," he cried.
>
> How blest are they who have not seen,
> and yet whose faith hath constant been,
> for they eternal life shall win.[11]

The use of this hymn annually can be a way of establishing a local Thomas Sunday "tradition," particularly if the other stanzas have been used on Easter Day.

Inasmuch as the First Day of the week that is designated as Thomas Sunday is also the Eighth Day of the resurrection, many layers of meaning are bound together with sufficient power to help ensure that Easter is not one day or week but a continuing occasion of seven weeks.

The Third Sunday of Easter: Meal Sunday

One manifestation of the Risen One surrounds the sharing of food. Jesus presides at table in the Emmaus home, and the two followers hasten to Jerusalem to tell those gathered there: "We have seen the Lord, who was made known to us in the breaking of bread." Later that evening Jesus appears in the room and, to dispel their fear that they are seeing a ghost, asks the disciples for something to eat. At the end of John's Gospel, the Risen One not only provides the apostles with a marvelous catch of fish but also prepares breakfast for them on the seashore. These stories interpret the presence of the Christ that we experience in the Eucharist, and are used as the respective Gospel readings on the Third Sunday of Easter in the three-year lectionary cycle. Hence this day can be called "Meal Sunday."

Some congregations see the Lord's Supper as a melancholy occasion, recalling primarily the upper room meal on Thursday evening (and only an exegetically limited interpretation of that). Using Meal Sunday as a eucharistic occasion can be a very helpful means for reorientation. This is particularly so in congregations that react to the proposal of having the Eucharist on Easter Day by asking in dismay: "But how can we possibly do anything so sad on a day that is supposed to be so happy?"

Particularly in connection with the Emmaus story, it can be very helpful to point out that at the table with the two after the resurrection, Jesus does the same things reported of him at the table with the Twelve before the crucifixion: takes bread, gives thanks, breaks the bread, and distributes it. Even though the Greek verbs are not absolutely identical in the two Lucan stories (22:14-19 and 24:30), they are so closely related that inescapably Luke seems to be insisting: "What happened in the upper room has been drastically and permanently altered in its significance as a result of the resurrection."

No longer is the sacrament simply a table in the valley of the shadow of death, prepared in the presence of one's enemies. This now is the banquet of heaven at which the victorious Paschal Lamb presides; it is the eternal Passover feast in which all rejoice in their deliverance from death and every other enemy by the power of God. Thus we, in the present, grasp with one hand the past and with the other the future, so that all of time intersects the eternity of God. The Eucharist as Emmaus meal of old, as present transforming experience, and as an anticipation of heaven is set forth boldly in a Wesley hymn text, with its many allusions to Luke 24:13-35:

> O Thou who this mysterious bread
> didst in Emmaus break,
> return, herewith our souls to feed,
> and to thy followers speak.
>
> Unseal the volume of thy grace,
> apply the gospel word;
> open our eyes to see thy face,
> our hearts to know the Lord.
>
> Of thee communing still, we mourn
> till thou the veil remove;
> talk with us, and our hearts shall burn
> with flames of fervent love.
>
> Enkindle now the heavenly zeal,
> and make thy mercy known,
> and give our pardoned souls to feel
> that God and love are one.[12]

The Fourth Sunday of Easter: Good Shepherd Sunday

In lectionary-based churches, in each of the three years of the cycle, a portion of John 10 is read on this Sunday, and Psalm 23 is invariably the Psalter; shepherding language occurs in the Epistles for Years A and C. While this may seem to be an innovation, it is in fact a recovery of ancient practice with a slight alteration in the timing. From the Easter sermons of Augustine, we know it was the custom in North Africa, at least, to use the Good Shepherd theme on the Third Sunday of Easter.

"Shepherd" as a metaphor for divine care seems to remain popular even in cultures that know almost nothing about the ways of sheep, or perhaps particularly in such cultures, given the romantic interpretations of what it means to be a shepherd. However that may be, the observance of Good Shepherd Sunday has current appeal.

But a particular concurrence of texts comes in Lectionary Year C, due to the reading from the Revelation, which refers twice to Christ as "Lamb." How can the lamb also be the shepherd? Or does that puzzle lead us directly into seemingly inherent contradictions about God that must be made: That the One we crucified and buried is alive? That the One we have hated loves us? That we are both sinful and justified before God, both dead in our sins and alive in Christ Jesus? While the assigned readings raise this issue only every third year, if Christ is truly our Paschal Lamb, then the lamb/shepherd puzzle is ever before us on this Sunday; and that may open expanded visions of the very nature of the God who is too great to be encapsuled by any human metaphor or title.

The Fifth Sunday of Easter: I AM Sunday

The title given to the day is derived from the Johannine readings. In Years A and B, two of the Gospel's "I am" sayings are used: "I am the way, the truth, and the life" and "I am the vine." In Year C, the reading from the Revelation proclaims "I am the Alpha and the Omega." While we tend to think of "I am" as grammatically routine material that precedes the "good stuff"—the actual identification that follows—in Johannine theology probably much more is at stake than that. In the multiple "I am" sayings of the Fourth Gospel and of the Revelation, likely there is a deliberate attempt to identify the Risen One as a manifestation of the same deity who announced to Moses from the burning bush: "I AM WHO I AM. Thus you shall say to the Israelites, 'I AM has sent me to you'" (Exod. 3:14).[13]

Assuming the plausibility of this interpretation, two things are implied: (1) John is asserting continuity between the Risen One and the God at the burning bush, even as in that Exodus account, the God who speaks to Moses asserts continuity with the One worshiped by Moses' ancestors. This Jesus who has been raised from the dead is not a new deity but rather a new revelation sent from, and consistent with, the God known of old. An American folk hymn enshrines this affirmation:

> To God and to the Lamb I will sing;
> To God and to the Lamb who is the great I AM,
> While millions join the theme I will sing.[14]

(2) The resurrection, like the theophany to Moses, is filled with profound mystery and a holy grandeur that must not be domesticated by our often limited imaginations. The "I AM" designation for God, even by the way it appears here in print, is unique to the extent that Jews refused to utter the title when coming across it in the Scriptures, but instead substituted another name for God entirely when reading aloud.[15] Thus we are put on notice that the resurrection, too, is something beyond our grasp, something before which we are to bow in awe, experiencing the joy but honoring the magnitude of divine grace. Thus this Sunday is in some ways a cautionary note in relation to last Sunday: Since the Good Shepherd is a metaphor to which we tend to "cozy up" with much familiarity, now we draw back a bit and remember that "I AM the Good Shepherd" has built into it a protection against a chumminess that can obscure the grandeur of the cosmic Christ.

The readings for this Sunday in each year of the cycle, of course, point to other meanings of the resurrection for the life of the church and thus provide each of the three years with a differing emphasis.

The Sixth Sunday of Easter

The Gospel readings for this Sunday prepare us for the observance of the Ascension by indicating both how Christians are to live together and by recalling the promises that the departure of the Lord into heaven is to be not a denial of the presence of the Risen One but a new mode of that presence in our midst. (This idea is amplified below in the discussion of the theological meaning of Ascension Day and the Day of Pentecost.) In the readings for this Sunday, Jesus speaks of the commandment that we are to love one another (particularly in Year A and B readings) and of the promise that the Spirit will work this love in us (particularly in Year A and C readings).

Apart from the affirmation about the work of the Spirit, the commandment to love readily becomes law rather than gospel. Any serious Christian knows how difficult it is truly to love others, and even the casual student of church history can illustrate this a thousand times over by citing most-distressing examples of the lack of charity among Christians and by Christians toward others across the centuries. That human beings have difficulty loving one another is beyond question. But the real question to be wrestled with today is,

"May it be that our real failure is that we have trusted in ourselves to achieve love when instead we should have accepted as a gift from the Spirit the love God showed to the world in the humiliation-exaltation of Jesus?"

The Seventh Sunday of Easter

In many congregations this day is observed not as the Seventh Sunday of Easter but as Ascension Sunday; for if no Ascension Day service is held on Thursday, its lectionary readings are transferred to the Sunday thereafter. Where the Seventh Sunday of Easter is kept as such, in lectionary churches the Gospel reading in each year is a portion of John 17—"the great high priestly prayer," in which Jesus commends the disciples to God, asking that "they all may be one" in order that the world may believe through them.

Thus this Sunday is an anticipation of next Sunday, when, on the Day of Pentecost, we hear of the company of Jesus' followers speaking one message, understood in every tongue; and, in the end, three thousand believe. But this Sunday is also a follow-up to the themes of Ascension Day. For the import of the ascension, as we are about to see, is that the world is not deprived of the presence of Christ by the ascent into heaven but is given that presence in a new and grander form, as implied in John 17.

The Ascension

In order to provide a more coherent commentary, Sundays Two through Seven of the Great Fifty Days have been discussed in sequence above. That procession of Sundays is, of course, interrupted by an important occasion on the fortieth day of Easter (hence, always a Thursday), which for centuries has marked the ascension of Jesus.

Current understandings of the universe, buttressed by the reign of reason in Western thought, have caused the ascension to become a large question mark for most Christians. It used to be supposed that heaven was a few thousand feet up in the air; now that we know something of the scope of the universe, this is manifest nonsense. Thus nagging questions about geography and physics come to the contemporary mind: How far would Jesus have had to go to get beyond the span of galaxies? Where is "heaven" anyhow? And given what we know about the mechanics of space travel, would not the body of Jesus have fried crisp due to friction while leaving the earth, or become a frozen block in the coldness of outer space? Lacking the sophisticated guidance systems made possible by modern computers, how did the body of Jesus avoid colliding with one of the zillion obstacles out there?

That contemporary people should ask such questions is unavoidable. That the contemporary church has dealt with them only by silence is unforgivable. In some quarters the silence has resulted in the loss of significant liturgical celebration. For many decades, large sectors of Protestantism simply did not observe Ascension Day, either on its proper Thursday or on the Sunday following. The occasion was too confusing and embarrassing. In other quarters the observance was kept, but with a tacit rule firmly understood: "Just commemorate this event and don't ask any questions about it. Keep science in one compartment of your mind and faith in another."

But even (or especially) in an age of sophisticated science, the ascension has crucial theological significance that cannot be readily surrendered, despite our scientific skepticism. In order to understand that significance, we must affirm above all that the ascension is an integral part of the resurrection, not something distinct from it. The ascension is observed separately for the sake of closer contemplation, not because it provides an independent set of meanings.[16] Originally, the great Paschal celebration of the church was a unified commemoration of the suffering, death, resurrection, and ascension of the Lord. Only several centuries after the birth of the church were the events divided into separate commemorations, with the ascension observance being moved to the fortieth day of Easter. The separation brings with it both an advantage and a difficulty.

The advantage of the separated observance is that it implies that the significance of the resurrection is too vast to be contemplated all at once. We divide this wonderful action of God into parts that we may the better approach the fullness of a mystery we can never fathom. The difficulty is that, failing to realize this, we lapse back into domesticating the resurrection. We think of it merely as a resuscitation, the reviving of a physical body, which (since it did not die again and have to be reburied, and since it is no longer around) must have escaped the earth and gone elsewhere. As a late colleague of mine, Professor Joseph Weber, used to complain, "Most contemporary Christians think the resurrection and ascension are a kind of two-stage rocket: The resurrection gets the body of Jesus up from the ground and then the ascension launches it into outer space." This understanding he bemoaned in the interest of a much richer interpretation that has to do not with the force of gravity and altitude but with basic and decisive attitudes about the continuing work of God in our world. So what does the ascension mean from this theological perspective? A great deal more than is generally supposed.

The Ascension Signals the Completion of God's Saving Work in Christ

The ascension first affirms that what God begins, God completes. The same Word of God that came from God to dwell among us returns to God. Ultimately this very Jesus "who has been taken up from you into heaven, will come in the same way as you saw him go" (Acts 1:11). That is to say, God is dependable. There is a unity to divine action that judges and countermands all the disunity and incompleteness of our mortal existence. It is a theme sounded again and again in those passages in John's Gospel sometimes called "the farewell discourses," in which Jesus promises that the Holy Spirit will complete all things announced in the incarnation.

Christ the Word, by whom all things were made and without whom nothing was made that came into existence (John 1:3), dwelt in the Godhead amidst the praise of angels. Now, the humiliation and suffering finished, the glory that was Christ's from the beginning is restored. The One who hung upon the cross, who was shown the greatest contempt and debased to the lowest ignominy human society could arrange, is once more exalted and given again the highest praise and greatest glory the heavenly throng can manage. In chapter 1 we imagined a scene in heaven when God asked the angels to volunteer to go to earth, but not one would come forward. Finally, it was none other than God who volunteered to suffer the humiliation. Now, thinking of resurrection and exaltation, we imagine another scene in heaven.

A sentinel angel creates a stir in the courts of heaven by announcing that the One who was incarnate is returning to the throne of God. Amid great excitement the eagerly awaited event occurs. The angels huddle around Christ and ask, "What was it like? Is it as bad down there as we fear it might be?" "Worse," comes the reply. "They actually crucified me." The heavenly host utters a collective gasp. "But you are back, safe and sound!" a cherub says boldly. "Yes," Christ answers. "Divine power overcame the worst they could do, and divine love is now in their midst always and everywhere." Then comes a voice from the throne: "Victorious is the Lamb that was slain. Blessed is the One who turned not aside the bitter cup, but drank it to the dregs. The night of suffering is ended. Come, enter into my joy." At this a sustained cheer resounds in heaven, and a great celebration begins. Music and dancing and feasting proclaim the return and exaltation of the humiliated One. The joy of reunion, the satisfaction of the completion of the work of salvation is proclaimed without restraint by angels and archangels as the celestial choirs sing: "Worthy is the Lamb who was slain to receive glory and blessing and honor and dominion and power, now and forever!" This is the first meaning of the ascension.

The Resurrection Is God's Raising Up of the Entire Fallen Creation

The ascension is a confirmation of human participation in the resurrection of Christ. That resurrection is not an event in which only one participates—Jesus; rather, the participation of Jesus in this great act of divine grace is a foretaste (prolepsis) of what is in store for all of God's creation. This is what Paul means not only by Christ as new creation but also by the apostolic assertion that "Christ has been raised from the dead, the first fruits of those who have died" (1 Cor. 15:20). The metaphor rests upon the timing of the resurrection of Jesus in relation to the beginning of the harvest on the third day of Passover: As the first swath of the sickle into the ripe grain signals the bounty of the full harvest that is about to be, so the raising of Jesus is a sure sign of the raising up of the whole fallen creation.

We today tend to suppose that from the beginning of time each righteous person, as death occurred, was admitted into heaven. But this was not the ancient view of things. Rather, it was believed that, except perhaps for a very few such as Enoch and Elijah, those who died entered a dismal place of shadowy existence—"Sheol." There they awaited their liberation. The Letter of 1 Peter takes up the story at that point: The eternal Christ (who cannot be destroyed by death), on the days between the entombment and the resurrection, went down into Sheol and "made a proclamation to the spirits in prison" (1 Pet. 3:19). Although the results of that proclamation are not made explicit, the implication is that the Good News had glorious effect: By the preaching of the cross those who lived before the crucifixion as well as those who lived after were given faith. The Letter to the Ephesians takes up the same theme but goes beyond the scope of Peter to connect this with the ascension: "When [scripture] says, 'He ascended,' what does it mean but that he had also descended into the lower parts of the earth? He who descended is the same one who ascended far above all the heavens, so that he might fill all things" (Eph. 4:9-10).[17]

In Orthodox Christianity there is a standard icon depicting the resurrection. Unlike Western art, which attempts to show post-resurrection appearances of the Lord set within familiar surroundings, the Eastern portrayal depicts Jesus in the underworld, standing atop the recently trampled gates of hell, beneath which the devil lies trapped. Holding in one hand the resurrection banner (a red cross upon the white field of a large pennant), with the other hand Christ reaches out to a vast host of waiting people. At the front of the line are Adam and Eve, righteous Abel, the Patriarchs, and David and Solomon; behind them huddles the whole of deceased humanity. Christ, "the New Adam," takes the hand of the first Adam, and thus begins what is about to become a grand, triumphal procession heavenward: Christ displaying the resurrection banner will lead the great parade into the gardens of Paradise regained.

If this seems to us a strange depiction of the resurrection, it is first because we have not read with understanding Ephesians 4:8, itself a citation of Psalm 68:18: "When he ascended on high he made captivity itself a captive" or, to use an older translation, "he led a host of captives" (RSV). But of greater consequence is the fact that we have failed to grasp that the resurrection is not simply about Christ but also about the whole of fallen creation. It is worth noting that the Greek word translated "resurrection" (*anastasis*), literally means "the standing up again." All that has "fallen" by virtue of disobedience now "stands up" again by virtue of grace. The ascension is that standing up again in its most dramatic form.

Nor should we in our anthropocentric arrogance assume that only we human beings participate with Christ in this resurrection. The New Testament view is cosmic: Christ is "the firstborn from the dead," whose resurrection signals the birth out of death of "all things, whether on earth or in heaven . . . through the blood of [the] cross" (Col. 1:18-20). Christ, ascending to glory, takes by the hand to heaven the whole of creation. Along with the once humiliated Jesus, whatever God has made is exalted, even as it was intended to be when, before the fall, God pronounced it "very good" (Gen. 1:31). Thus the work of God in both the new and the old creation is exalted to the heavens; and from thence shall come forth the new heaven and new earth when the fullness of the power of the resurrection can be revealed at the end of time. (See Rev. 1:5 and 21:1.)

We Are Assured of the Permanence of Human Experience in the Heart of God

The ascension further means that in returning to God, the Risen One takes along the fullness of human life experienced by Jesus, including the worst of earthly agony. Christians have no good reason for doubting that God understands in the most personal possible way our human struggle, sorrows, and defeats. The God who came into our midst as a baby and dwelt among us experienced all things, even to the most severe forms of oppression and suffering; that experience was not a transitory episode to be forgotten by God after thirty years. No, that experience is carried into heaven, that we may know the Most High identifies always even with the least and the lowest.

That is the import of what is otherwise to us the strange language of the Letter to the Hebrews:

> For it is clear that [Jesus] did not come to help angels, but the descendants of Abraham. Therefore he had to become like his brothers and sisters in every respect, so that he might be a merciful and faithful high priest in the service of God, to make a sacrifice of atonement for the sins of the people. Because he himself was tested by what he suffered, he is able to help those who are being tested. (2:16-18)

> Since, then, we have a great high priest who has passed through the heavens, Jesus, the Son of God, let us hold fast to our confession [of

faith]. For we do not have a high priest who is unable to sympathize with our weaknesses, but we have one who in every respect has been tested as we are, yet without sin. Let us therefore approach the throne of grace with boldness, so that we may receive mercy and find grace to help in time of need. (4:14-16)

When celebrated in its fullness, the ascension is a source of great strength to all who suffer.

By the Power of the Holy Spirit, the Risen One Is Unconfined by Time and Space

Finally, the ascension is an affirmation that the Risen One is now bound by neither time nor space. Jesus of Nazareth dwelt some thirty years in a very small territory to the east of the Mediterranean. But through the power of the resurrection Christ is revealed as being present at all times and in all places. That presence is effected by the power of the Holy Spirit, which is nothing less than Christ filling all things. Failure to appreciate this meaning of the resurrection gives rise to two misunderstandings that are widespread, even among the most devout.

The first misunderstanding is seen in a lament such as this from devout Christians: "Wouldn't it be wonderful if we could have lived back in Jesus' time and listened to him teach! How much more fortunate were his disciples in that regard than we are." In addition to dismissing the Gospels' portrayals of the disciples as dolts who could comprehend almost nothing until after the resurrection, this attitude wrongly assumes that the power of God was more present to human beings before the ascension than since.

The second misunderstanding is revealed in the desire of many Christians to travel to Israel on the assumption that they will be "closer to Jesus" at the sites of events in his life. While there are a number of valid reasons for making such a pilgrimage, this particular reason, as fully as the desire to have lived in Jesus' time, fails to grasp what the ascension is about. Both stances, while deeply sincere, seem unaware of the New Testament depiction of Jesus Christ as "the firstborn of all creation" in whom "all things in heaven and on earth were created" and in whom "all things hold together" (Col.

71

1:15, 16, 17). And the ascension as theological doctrine undergirds precisely such an understanding of the cosmic work of Christ.

It would be difficult to find a finer or more accessible interpretation of the third and fourth meanings of the ascension than in this hymn text by Brian Wren:

> Christ is alive! Let Christians sing.
> His cross stands empty to the sky.
> Let streets and homes with praises ring.
> His love in death shall never die.
>
> Christ is alive! No longer bound
> to distant years in Palestine,
> he comes to claim the here and now
> and dwell in every place and time.
>
> Not throned afar, remotely high,
> untouched, unmoved by human pains,
> but daily, in the midst of life,
> our Savior in the Godhead reigns.
>
> In every insult, rift, and war,
> where color, scorn, or wealth divide,
> he suffers still, yet loves the more,
> and lives, though ever crucified.
>
> Christ is alive, and comes to bring
> good news to this and every age,
> till earth and all creation ring
> with joy, with justice, love, and praise.[18]

When the ascension is celebrated in light of the four meanings above, it ceases to be seen as an event problematic in terms of geography or physics and becomes an unfolding of the practical consequences of the resurrection; and thus the ascension is something to be celebrated in the church with great thanksgiving.

The Final Sunday of Easter: The Day of Pentecost

For those who use the commonly agreed upon three-year lectionary, on every Sunday of Easter a selection is read from the book of the Acts. On Easter Day the reading in all years is Acts 10:34-43. On subsequent Sundays the readings are from Acts 2:14 onward throughout the book. What seems at first a curious fact is that only at the end of the Great Fifty Days is Acts 2:1-21 read. In other words, the season seems to trace the formation of the church through time but only on the very last Sunday reports the birth of the church on the Day of Pentecost. From the perspective of logic, this seems unjustified until two things are understood.

First, the ordering is theological, not chronological: Reading from the Acts throughout the Great Fifty Days is a sturdy affirmation that the church is built upon the resurrection and its proclamation by people of faith. The resurrection is central, not subsidiary, to the formation and growth of the church. To put it another way: The formation of the church is an immediate consequence of the resurrection, not a delayed reaction to it; therefore, we cannot wait until seven weeks after Easter morning to contemplate what it means to be church.

Second, the Day of Pentecost is a summarizing occasion, not an inaugural occasion. Contrary to understandings in the past (which saw this Day as the beginning of a new season called "Whitsuntide" or "the Season of Pentecost"), now the Day of Pentecost is viewed as it was in ancient times, as the closing of the annual Easter festival. As such, the Day of Pentecost is an occasion for recapitulation. And no New Testament passage so fully recapitulates the nature of the church in the power of the Spirit as does Acts 2:1-21.

Beyond these practical concerns related to lectionary design, however, are other basic considerations. The Holy Spirit is the agent whereby the Risen Christ is made present to the church. The Day of Pentecost does not mark the beginning of the Holy Spirit's work in the world, as is sometimes wrongly supposed. (Only Luke describes the events of this Day, and in Luke's Gospel the Holy Spirit is at work from the very first chapter onward, beginning with the angelic announcement of the births of John the Baptizer and Jesus; see 1:15, 35.) Luke is clear that the Spirit of God is ever active in creation. What is "new" about Pentecost is that this same Spirit who has worked in many ways now constitutes the church of God.

Thus the Day of Pentecost in Christian worship is primarily about the church as corporate community. The Day is, to use the terms of formal theology, "ecclesiological in focus." That is, this Day is not about the work of the Spirit in the hearts of individual believers; there is ample opportunity to deal with that work throughout the year. The Day of Pentecost is about the formation of the church out of a frightened band of followers; that tight-lipped crowd, which had huddled timidly behind closed doors, is thrust by the Spirit into the streets of Jerusalem to proclaim the gospel in terms everyone can understand. How are we to account for this change? Only by recognizing that the Spirit is the One who forms the church by making the Risen Christ manifest in power.

That formation has to do with us as clearly as with the apostolic band twenty centuries ago. Still the Spirit mediates to the church the Resurrection Presence unfettered by time or space, so that we who are timid in the faith may become the community of faith, boldly witnessing in the world. This, then, is the church's memory and petition on the Day of Pentecost:

> Filled with the Spirit's power, with one accord
> the infant church confessed its risen Lord.
> O Holy Spirit, in the church today
> no less your power of fellowship display.[19]

Given the nature of the occasion as the closing of the most joyous season of the church, the Day of Pentecost deserves to be celebrated more enthusiastically than often is the case. In those years when the dating of this Day coincides with Mother's Day or Memorial Day weekend, in no case should the church's witness to the presence and power of Christ's Spirit be obscured by themes derived from the civil calendar. While it cannot command the same liturgical attention as Easter Day, the closing day of the Great Fifty Days should be a distinctive observance, anticipated eagerly each year by worshiping congregations. It is an excellent time for baptism and its reaffirmation, and certainly an occasion for the festival observance of the eucharistic banquet of the church.

The unifying effect of the Spirit's work can be proclaimed liturgically in interesting ways. Where members of the congregation are fluent in various languages, after the reading of Acts 2 the Gospel lesson can be read in sequence in several languages other than English. Then this passage can be read in English either by one

74

person or by the congregation, if printed in a bulletin with great care to ensure that the format facilitates unison reading.

Another possibility is to set in dramatic juxtaposition the story of the tower of Babel (Gen. 11:1-9) and Acts 2. In the Babel account human pride and presumption result in a divided humanity, beset by confusion and misunderstanding; but this is reversed by divine action when, on the Day of Pentecost, people from many places understand and accept the same proclamation of grace. The Babel account can be read first in its entirety in English, but then be read a second time, with the English reader being joined every few words by someone reading in another language. As one tongue after another joins in, the result is the kind of linguistic cacophony the narrative itself reports. When all readers finish the Genesis account, after a brief silence the Acts 2 account can be read in English by a single reader or by all of the readers in unison (though the latter requires a great deal of practice, especially if the catalog of hearers in 2:9-11 is not to become chaotic).[20]

Either form of the reading of Acts 2 may well be followed by the singing of these stanzas:

> Come, sinners, to the gospel feast;
> let every soul be Jesus' guest.
> Ye need not one be left behind,
> for God hath bid all humankind.
>
> Sent by my Lord, on you I call;
> the invitation is to all.
> Come, all the world! Come, sinner, thou!
> All things in Christ are ready now.[21]

Seen as the undoing of the curse of Babel, the Day of Pentecost (with or without the Genesis 11 reading) is a crucial means of reinforcing the notion that this day is about the church as the community of the Spirit, not merely about the work of the Spirit in the hearts of individuals. Babel results in disconnectedness, in a confused individualism. The church implies reconnectedness, such as that set forth in Paul's metaphor of the church as a body having many parts, each different but in need of the others (1 Cor. 12:4-31).

The need for a theology about the Day of Pentecost is seen by reflecting on how readily Christians misunderstand the nature of the church. For many people the church is a voluntary organization of individuals and exists primarily for reasons that relate to efficiency. Concerning worship, for example, it is tacitly suspected that in principle each Christian household could stay at home and have a pastor come to them to instruct them, administer the sacraments, and so on. But this would be too costly and probably would require more clergy than could be recruited. So it is more efficient for a number of households to contract together, and to establish a central meeting place and time at which the scriptures can be interpreted and the sacraments administered by someone trained in these tasks. Further, since most worship gives a central place to music, it is more effective to have a number of people sing with the support of a choir and a good musical instrument than for four or five people in a home to attempt to sing, probably unaccompanied. Because such a gathering is purely voluntary, people feel free to participate when they wish (particularly when they "need" to "get something out of it"), and to do otherwise the rest of the time.

A proper theology of the Day of Pentecost says a resounding "No!" to such popular ideas. The church is a community called together by the Spirit of the Risen One. It is not something we choose to do (and equally well could choose not to do), but something to which we are summoned. The Greek word for church (*ekklēsia* from which we derive "ecclesiastical") means "those who have been called forth or summoned," much as one is summoned to appear in a court of law. And we are called as a body of interdependent parts, not as separable individuals. The free-spirited individualism of our age is a manifestation of Babel, not Pentecost, as should be evident from the intransigent divisions and intractable conflicts such individualism fosters. The Risen One, who is present at all times and in all places, seeks to bind together by the action of the Spirit all things that have been wrongly separated. Participation therefore is not something we do on the basis of personal choice or need; participation in the Body of Christ is inherent in being Christian. The church, not the individual, is the irreducible unit of Christianity. Further, the church is to be a sign of the future: No matter how haltingly and imperfectly, the church seeks to enact in the present world the justice

76

and grace that characterize the eternal reign of God. Therefore Christians participate in the church not so much for what they can get as for what they can give, for what they can offer as an alternative to the dominant ways of the world.

Easter Day: The Great Sunday

Only now that we have considered the season as a whole can we discuss Easter Day itself; for that day is an inaugural occasion and can be understood only in light of what is to be inaugurated. In other words, the entire season of the Great Fifty Days defines the opening day. So rich is the season that its first day cannot sound all of the seasonal themes; but like an overture in music, Easter Day establishes the tone of what is to follow. Easter Day should be a bursting forth of faith, a kind of explosion that opens congregations to an experience of divine mystery and that moves the worshiper beyond the domesticated understandings of resurrection discussed in chapter 1.

For most congregations, the central observance of Easter Day occurs at some point between nine in the morning and noon; where it is customary that such a service last no longer than seventy-five minutes (and that every choir sing an anthem), constraints upon an ample proclamation of the Resurrection should be obvious. Among many Protestants, an earlier service at or shortly after dawn and held out-of-doors (when possible) is a local tradition. It is usually assumed that such a "sunrise" service is not a substitute for the later service, but that people will attend both, thereby providing some opportunity for the expansion of themes.

Increasingly popular in many locales is a Vigil Service, an impressive rite that provides much more ample opportunity for an unhurried and concentrated proclamation of the resurrection than do the services later on Easter Day. The Vigil best serves the faithful who have attended regularly during Lent and likewise will attend throughout the Great Fifty Days. For by its design, the Vigil recapitulates Lenten themes and announces Easter themes. Because the Vigil is the final portion of the Triduum at the conclusion of Lent, its consideration in more detail is found in the next chapter.

However celebrated, the rites of Easter Day should accord with the hymn of Luther:

77

Christ Jesus lay in death's strong bands
for our offenses given;
but now at God's right hand he stands,
and brings us life from heaven;
wherefore let us joyful be,
and sing to God right thankfully
loud songs of Alleluia. Alleluia!

It was a strange and dreadful strife
when life and death contended;
the victory remained with life;
the reign of death was ended.
Stripped of power, no more it reigns,
an empty form alone remains;
death's sting is lost forever! Alleluia!

Here the true Paschal Lamb we see,
whom God so freely gave us;
he died on the accursed tree—
so strong his love!—to save us.
See, his blood doth mark our door.
Faith points to it; death passes o'er;
and Satan cannot harm us. Alleluia!

So let us keep the festival
whereto the Lord invites us;
Christ is himself the joy of all,
the Sun that warms and lights us.
By his grace he doth impart
eternal sunshine to the heart;
the night of sin is ended! Alleluia!

Then let us feast this Easter day
on the true bread of heaven;
the Word of grace hath purged away
the old and wicked leaven.
Christ alone our souls will feed;
he is our meat and drink indeed;
faith lives upon no other. Alleluia![22]

4

Lent: Forty Days of Devotion and Discipline

First, a numerical puzzle. That Lent consists of forty days is rather well known. But go to a calendar; count beginning on Ash Wednesday and ending with the day before Easter. The result? Not forty days but forty-six days! Why? Because the forty days of Lent are fast days in the broad sense, times of discipline and self-restraint. But as we have seen, the Lord's Day is ever a feast within the church. Therefore in order to have forty days of fasting, six Sundays must be excluded from the count. Lent in truth is forty weekdays plus six Lord's Days.[1]

Why forty days? In biblical terms forty is a round number symbolizing fullness—a span of time sufficient to accomplish what needs to take place; as such the number is used frequently and becomes a kind of shorthand for much of sacred history. Rain fell in Noah's time for forty days and nights; for this same period of time Moses and Elijah (who represent respectively the Law and the Prophets) dwelt at Horeb; for forty days Jesus endured temptation in the wilderness and later for the same period was revealed to the disciples after the resurrection. Nineveh was given forty days in which to repent. For forty years Israel wandered in the wilderness prior to admission into the promised land. Eli was a judge over Israel for forty years, and Saul, David, and Solomon are reported to have had reigns of forty years each.

In the early centuries, forty days was the time sufficient for converts to make their final, intensive preparation for baptism; and thus a pattern for Lent developed.[2] So also the ancient baptismal preparation dictated this period to be a time of particular devotion and discipline, especially of the prayer and fasting commended in Acts 14:23 (and Matthew 17:21 and Mark 9:29 in older translations). Jesus' own preparation for ministry by fasting forty days in the

79

desert exerted great influence, despite the obvious difference that Jesus engaged in this practice after baptism while those converting to the Christian faith came to keep the forty fast days prior to their baptism.

In a number of languages the days of Lent are referred to as "the Fast" or as "the Forty."[3] We shall shortly consider what fasting means and how it applies to spirituality today. But more must be said about the season before that aspect of its discipline can be considered.

The Foci of the Season

Briefly put, Lent is like an ellipse: It is a single entity with a double focus. The Forty Days are (a) a time for a probing consideration of our human condition, including sin and its deadly consequences for both individuals and society, and (b) a time for an equally intense consideration of the new possibilities offered to us in Jesus Christ and their implications for practical living. Both foci determine the shape of the season as a whole. But in a sense our Lenten journey takes us through the ellipse lengthwise. At the start of Lent (whose tone is set by Ash Wednesday), we are more fully aware of disobedience as our focus. By the close of the Forty Days (whose tone is set by Palm-Passion Sunday and the approach of the Triduum), we are more keenly attuned to the benefits of divine redemption. We begin by stressing penitence: an acknowledgment of our rebellion against God and our alienation from God's whole creation. We move on to the fruits of repentance: the amendment of life that results when we turn around and by God's grace head in a new direction.

The process is intended to engage persons at quite different stages of commitment. At least three groups merit consideration. (1) We have noted how Lent came to be formed in relation to converts' final preparation for baptism. (2) But for the baptized who are active in the life of the church there is ever the need for reassessment and renewal, lest a lively faith be diminished by an increased conformity to old ways, or simply by the dead weight of unimaginative piety. (3) Finally, for those who have departed from the faith ("backslidden" to use an old pietistic term), the Forty Days can be a time for restitution and restoration. The existence of the second group of people is usually acknowledged and dealt with in varying ways. In much of American Protestantism the periodic "revival meeting" (whether held in Lent or at some other time) is primarily for this group. As the name indicates, the revival is less an evangelistic occasion directed at the uncommitted than it is a time to revive the sagging spirits of those who are active. Other forms of reinvigorating the weary abound for those in this second category. But the first and third categories of people often get little attention.

With respect to the first group: Until recently we have gotten by with assuming that by virtue of a pervasive "Christian" ethos in our society, uncommitted adults who wanted to come into the church needed only a bit of orientation. Three or four classes of an hour each (often conducted by the pastor) would cover the basics of Christian doctrine, church history, denominational polity, and parish programs. That would do it. But it no longer will (and never did, if we are honest). In our day there are adults without a significant working knowledge of Christianity who feel their need for a deep and engaging faith. They are not served well by four or five hours of passively enduring "instruction"; and the more thoughtful of them will not put up with it. Intuitively they sense that the Christian faith implies a vast alteration of values and an intense participation in mission, and they will seek out congregations that both expect much from them and offer them clear direction and sustained support.

The third group, the "backsliders," have all but been abandoned by the church. Their names are periodically expunged from the active membership rolls with the explanation that they are "no longer interested." Often this conclusion is reached because they have not made donations of record in a specified number of years.

Might not the Forty Days bring all three groups together? The active Christians may well find their own faith reinvigorated by joining in the process of helping to prepare others for baptism and in visiting and encouraging a renewal of faith in those who seem to have disappeared from the congregation. For each group, a somewhat different pattern of devotion and discipline will be appropriate; yet the dual Lenten foci of considering both our human condition and the transforming power God offers will apply to the needs of all.

However these Forty Days are ordered locally, their observance should be disciplined—that is, intentional and sustained; and that discipline should proceed not from a sense of duty or obligation but from a sense of grateful devotion. In the past much was made of "giving up something" for Lent. At times this was a trivial if harmless self-denial: abstaining from chocolate or attendance at movies. At times it was dishonest: giving up cigarettes because the physician had sternly warned of the dangers of smoking, or reducing food intake because weight loss was desired. In reaction, it has now come into vogue to suggest that instead we should "take on something" for Lent: pay a visit each week to someone who is ill or shut in, add an additional passage of scripture or prayer to personal devotions, or increase charitable offerings for six weeks. None of these is reprehensible; but neither do these grasp the depth of what is meant by Lenten devotion and discipline, if for no other reason than that they are temporary; presumably once Easter arrives, these "add-ons" will be set aside for another forty-six weeks.

The fuller Lenten discipline is a self-examination that seeks greater conformity to the mind of Christ, and more effective ministry on behalf of the world (which is what true devotion is all about). In this perspective, Lenten disciplines are not temporary deletions or additions but spiritual exercises that permanently alter us. A budding pianist at a certain stage spends hours practicing scales, and the novice typist again and again keys in: "The quick brown fox jumps over the lazy dog." Far from being exercises of only temporary value or even busywork, these disciplines actually alter neural pathways such that years later access to the resulting skills can be gained with only a minimum of effort. By the same logic it is said that once you have learned, you can never quite forget how to ride a bicycle.

Solid spiritual disciplines seek to effect the same kind of permanent acquisition. Instead of forbidding chocolate or adding a Bible reading for six-and-a-half weeks, Lenten disciplines drive deeply into the religious psyche by asking questions such as these:

- What progress am I making in sharing gladly what I have with others, particularly with the stranger and the poor?
- What attitudes do I convey to those who irritate me? How can awareness of my own need of God's grace enable me to be more gracious to them?

- How has my sense of interconnectedness in corporate worship grown of late, and how can I move ahead in appreciating the contributions and needs of other members in the congregation to which I belong?
- Am I as charitable and thoughtful to family members as to others? Or do I "take it out" on my family when life at school or work gets hectic?
- Can I redistribute my long-range personal budget in order to have more money to give away?
- When I hear someone being unjustly maligned, do I speak up to correct the record, or am I a silent accomplice?
- How can I more effectively and consistently support legislation and social programs that help the disadvantaged rather than hurt them?
- In devotional acts of prayer and reading, am I increasing my attention span and discovering new ways of listening rather than of talking, of giving thanks rather than of complaining?
- As I uncover and attempt to deal with one level of prejudice in my life, what other levels do I find lurking underneath, and how can I confront them?
- In addition to intercessory prayer, what habits can I develop that allow me to be more responsive to the sick, the distressed, and the bereaved, particularly when their needs emerge suddenly and require immediate attention? Can I plan spaces into my life to allow for such unanticipated opportunities to minister to others?
- Am I, by consistent attendance at worship, a witness to others of the worthiness of the God I follow? Or am I, by my sporadic attendance, suggesting that God is worth serving some times, but not others?

These and similar disciplines are designed to have effects far past the Lenten season and indeed are intended to produce new pathways of devotion and discipline in the same way that the exercises of the pianist or typist create new and enduring neural pathways.

It is in this same context that the ancient practice of fasting is best understood. Fasting is not primarily about giving up something; and certainly it should not result from a notion that our physical needs are unimportant or that the satisfaction of a pleasant meal is to be despised as being too self-indulgent. Fasting can alert us, however, to unacknowledged obsessions we may have about eating that can be tamed or redirected. Fasting can powerfully remind us of our dependence on God and others: Were it not for the One who gives seed to the sower, and for those who plant and harvest, and mill the grain into flour, who bake the bread, and deliver it to the store, we would be permanently hungry out of circumstance, not temporarily hungry out of choice. Hunger should also cultivate within us a great understanding for the plight of the underfed and for the anxiety and anger that drive them to social unrest and rebellion. A fast can also be to us a revelation as to how much time we normally use for food purchasing, preparation, consumption, and cleanup; that in turn raises the questions, "To what good use can I put the time saved while on the fast?" and "Over the long haul, can I streamline these tasks in order to have more hours available for Christian service?"

Lest Lenten discipline and devotion lead to smugness or a false sense of spiritual security, it must be noted that all such endeavors depend on grace. We do not save ourselves by virtue of such spiritual exercises; rather, we seek simply to alleviate the blockages that prevent God from acting freely in and through us. As we have been insisting that the meaning of the Great Fifty Days must be mastered before considering the nature of the Forty Days, as a corollary we must note that all Lenten devotion and discipline presupposes our place in the new creation inaugurated by Christ. The confession of Paul is a worthy motto for every serious Christian:

> I died to the law, so that I might live to God. I have been crucified with Christ; and it is no longer I who live, but it is Christ who lives in me. And the life I now live in the flesh I live by faith in the Son of God, who loved me and gave himself for me. (Gal. 2:19-20)

The design of the Forty Days is intended precisely to facilitate and reinforce this conviction within us.

Opening the Season: Ash Wednesday and the First Sunday

In some ways the solemnity of Ash Wednesday exceeds that of Good Friday; for the latter centers on redemption (which is why it is called "good"), but the former is primarily a confrontation with unregenerate and therefore thoroughly unpleasant reality. Often the

Ash Wednesday rites begin with (or elsewhere include) the plaintive call of Joel the prophet:

> Blow the trumpet in Zion;
>   sound the alarm on my holy mountain!
> Let all the inhabitants of the land tremble,
>   for the day of the LORD is coming, it is near—
> a day of darkness and gloom,
>   a day of clouds and thick darkness! . . .
> Yet even now, says the LORD,
>   return to me with all your heart,
> with fasting, with weeping, and with mourning. (Joel 2:1-2, 12)

The crux of the rites for Ash Wednesday is in the formula spoken at the imposition of ashes: "Remember, O mortal, that you are dust; and to dust you shall return" (Gen. 3:19).

Ash Wednesday is intended to be a bold confrontation with death. This is to many in our world a painful dose of reality; for we live in a culture that prefers to ignore death to the fullest extent possible and to dress up that which cannot be concealed. The dying are often sequestered in medical care facilities; and their corpses are displayed in finery and exquisite coffins, but only after the morticians and cosmeticians have done their best to make the dead bodies look youthful and vibrant. Then comes the church and declares brashly once a year: "Face it. You will die and your body will decay. You are powerless to prevent it, and denial will get you nowhere. Even the finest medical technology can do nothing to change the fact that the death rate is exactly what it has always been—one per person. So stop kidding yourself!"

This harsh medicine of reality is intended to set in motion a reconsideration of the meaning of life and death—apart from Christ and in Christ. Ashes, the sign of death, are put on the forehead not in some random pattern but in the shape of a cross.[4] This alters the starkness of the message, which thus becomes: "You will die. You cannot change that. But you can die in Christ, whose death transforms your own demise. Meanwhile, live in Christ and discover Christ's new life, which conquers death." It is significant that in the Ash Wednesday service we do not stop reading Joel 2 at verse 12. We continue: "Return to the LORD, your God, / [who] is gracious

85

and merciful, / slow to anger, and abounding in steadfast love, / and relents from punishing" (2:13). If the Supper of the Lord is celebrated as a part of the Ash Wednesday service, that becomes for us the strengthening, nourishing table prepared in the midst of our enemies, assuring us that we can pass through the darkest valley without fear and find our place at the great resurrection feast in the house of the Lord.

The First Sunday in Lent amplifies the themes of the previous Wednesday. In Year A we hear the ancient story of transgression in Eden; but following immediately is Psalm 32 with its opening reassurance: "Happy are those whose transgression is forgiven, / whose sin is covered." Then come Paul's words about trespasses, divine judgment, and the free gift of righteousness through Christ. Year B recalls the gracious covenant after the flood in Noah's day, with assurances from 1 Peter 3 that our resurrection with Christ, signified in baptism, is consonant with all prefigured in the ark. In Year C, the Hebraic creed of Deuteronomy 26 reminds us of the necessity and accessibility of divine grace, and Paul assures us that no sinner who believes in Christ will be put to shame, for "everyone who calls on the name of the Lord shall be saved" (Rom. 10:13).

In all three years, the Gospel reading recounts the faithfulness of Jesus, who steadfastly resisted all temptation in the desert; and thereby we are to understand that the One who was thus tempted stands ready to strengthen us and bring us triumphant through all trials.

Thus the first five days of the Forty proclaim both judgment and hope. We cannot escape who we are: rebellious and mortal. But we are assured of what we may become by the grace of God: redeemed and raised from death. Thus we are propelled on a journey toward Jerusalem—both a six weeks' journey and a pilgrimage that will last to our final breath; a journey both to the earthly, temporal city in which Jesus will die and arise and to that heavenly, eternal city in which all tears will be wiped from our eyes and death will be no more.

The Second Through the Fifth Sundays in Lent

For those who follow the common lectionary, the themes of the four interior Sundays in Lent vary from week to week and year to year; and yet a common body of considerations persists. The variety and continuity is best seen by a schematic overview in which the themes of the Old Testament, Epistle, and Gospel readings for each week are summarized.

Year A	Year B	Year C
Second Sunday		
Covenant with Abram	Promise to Abram and Sarai	Abram's vision
Abraham's faith; grace	Abraham's faith and ours	We await a Savior; stand firm
Nicodemus and Jesus	Take up your cross	"How often I would have gathered you"
Third Sunday		
Water from the rock	The Decalogue given	Come to the waters; buy without price
Justification by grace	The cross as foolishness	Israel's "baptism"; do not be idolaters
Woman at the well	Cleansing the temple	The fig tree spared
Fourth Sunday		
Anointing of David	Serpent in the wilderness	Entering Canaan
Walk in the light	Saved by grace	The New Creation
The man born blind	God so loved the world	The prodigal and elder sons
Fifth Sunday		
Valley of the dry bones	Covenant in the heart	"I do a new thing"
Life in the Spirit	Christ as high priest forever	The past is over; Christ is all
Raising of Lazarus	"I will draw all to myself"	Mary anoints Jesus

Although specific configurations vary from year to year, all years share common motifs. One is covenant: God's gracious initiative and promise on which we can depend and to which we are called to respond with joyful and sustained obedience. Another theme is the newness of life offered by transforming grace, particularly as this is focused in the cross. In Year A ancient allusions to baptism abound (reference to "water and the Spirit" in the Nicodemus narrative; water from the rock at Rephidim, and living water offered to the woman at the well; anointing and enlightenment, which confer new status to the baptized; the resurrection life in the Spirit by which the baptized live).[5]

The schematic overview above reveals clearly that while the saving work of Christ upon the cross is not excluded from consideration, until the final Sunday of the Forty Days this theme enters more by allusion and promise than by explicit reference. Certainly Lent is not six-and-a-half weeks of marching around the foot of Mount Calvary. Rather, this season engages us in the process of confronting who we are by nature, who we are by God's purpose and redeeming action, and what we can become by divine grace. To use the formal vocabulary of theology: Lent is a recapitulation of our understanding of creation and the fall, and of regeneration and sanctification.

To summarize the basics of the faith each year is necessary for those about to be baptized, and highly useful to those already baptized but in need of recommitment or even of restoration to the faith after having lapsed as conscientious Christians. Ash Wednesday and the First Sunday in Lent set the course for the journey. The interior Sundays propel us forward so that finally we do find our feet planted at the base of the cross, with our eyes gazing beyond to behold the power of the resurrection and to seek its manifestations even now in our daily discipleship.

The Sixth Sunday and Days Following

Palm-Passion Sunday

The final Sunday of the Forty Days is known by various titles; but almost nowhere is it any longer simply "Palm Sunday," in either name or recommended manner of observance. The basic reason is this: To separate out the narratives of the entry of Jesus into the city and interpret the occasion behind them as utterly joyous and victorious is to misread the Gospels. The label "triumphal entry" is a misnomer and a source of much misinterpretation. The New Testament writers know fully well that the "Hosanna!" cries of Sunday will by Friday turn into the calls for crucifixion. The entry into the city is charged with irony, and it is about us as fully as it is about the people of ancient Jerusalem: Our faith, too, is fickle; we are the crucifiers of the One whose coming we have called "blessed." (Hence our withered palm branches will produce the dust applied to our foreheads next Ash Wednesday.) Jesus enters the city for one reason only: to die. The Gospel writers are clear about this, and "Palm Sunday" observances that are "three cheers for Jesus" forfeit biblical integrity.

Second, if there was a time when the full Sunday morning congregation could be counted on to return on Thursday and Friday of Holy Week to hear the rest of the story, that time is long gone. The next appearance for most will occur on Easter morning. Since the Easter liturgy is almost certainly a "rah-rah" event, if the prior Lord's Day has the same tone, those who attend only on Sundays receive a very distorted view of reality. The church is constrained to insist that there is no route to an empty tomb except by way of the cross.

Thus the Sunday before Easter is distinguished by being the only lectionary occasion for which two Gospel readings and two psalms are appointed. The first Gospel passage, the story of the entry, is intended to be read at the very beginning of the service, as the palm branches are blessed and distributed. Then the congregation joins in Psalm 118:1-2, 19-29 and sings a hymn such as "All Glory, Laud, and Honor." But almost immediately thereafter the day's liturgy takes a sharp turn. Isaiah 50:4-9*a* (a portion of one of the "servant" songs) is read. Psalm 31:1-16 follows, with its plaintive cry:

> Be gracious to me, O LORD, for I am in distress;
>   my eye wastes away from grief,
>   my soul and body also.
> For my life is spent with sorrow,
>   and my years with sighing;
> my strength fails because of my misery,
>   and my bones waste away.
>
> I am the scorn of all my adversaries,
>   a horror to my neighbors,
> an object of dread to my acquaintances;
>   those who see me in the street flee from me.
> I have passed out of mind like one who is dead;
>   I have become like a broken vessel. (Ps. 31:9-12)

Then comes a reading of the humiliation-exaltation hymn of Philippians 2 concerning the One who became obedient to death, followed by a reading of one of the passion accounts (varying with the year, and with options given as to length). All of this places us at the cross. No "Palm Sunday" hymns are appropriate thereafter, but only texts such as "When I Survey the Wondrous Cross" or "O Sacred Head Now Wounded." And the sermon for the day centers on Golgotha, not the procession into the city. The departing congregation is left to ponder the wonder of God's generosity in the face of human depravity and the possibility of human transformation as a result of divine grace.

Monday, Tuesday, and Wednesday of Holy Week

After the final Sunday of the Forty Days, few congregations gather again until Thursday. The three intervening days serve primarily as times for personal contemplation. This is not to discourage the scheduling of corporate worship; but where that is not feasible, the lectionary readings for these days may be published in the church newsletter and Sunday bulletin, so that the lections can be used at home. All readings for these days are related to the passion and crucifixion.

Whether Monday, Tuesday, and Wednesday are observed in the home or as a part of congregational worship, they can be valuable times of both consolidation and preparation. By way of consolidation, these are days to review the entire Lenten journey. From the death sentence of Eden spoken on Ash Wednesday, the faithful have moved through six weeks of devotion and disciplined examination, arriving on the final Sunday at Calvary. Thus our death *by* sin is incorporated into Christ's death *for* sin.

A durable old legend held that Jesus was crucified directly over the place where Adam and Eve were buried. Many artists, depicting the crucifixion, showed a human skull at the foot of the cross, with the blood of the savior streaming upon it. Historical fact this is not; and yet it is worthy theology: We who are dead by our sins are made alive by One who knew no sin. We have had whispered in our ears on Ash Wednesday the ancient death sentence of Eden—"You are dust, and to dust you shall return." Having worked our way through the implications of both sin and grace, we have come at last to One whose flesh is given "for the life of the world" (John 6:51), and thus for us.

Now we arrive at the liturgical observance that both culminates Lent and inaugurates Easter, a single service that stretches across three days with extended interruptions but no diminution of unity. To that, the most holy service of the year, we are now ready to turn.

Triduum: Three Days, One Act of Worship

As just intimated, the service that begins on the evening of Holy Thursday with footwashing and the Supper of the Lord is best thought of as a single worship event that is completed only by the announcement of the resurrection and its celebration at the Easter Vigil on Saturday evening or early Sunday morning. This unified service occurs in at least three separate time periods, with the intermediate one being the afternoon or evening of Good Friday.

In the early church all was done in a single extended service; the separation into parts did not evolve into its present form for centuries. And until recently the division into parts destroyed the ancient sense of unity; the strange title for these services is an attempt to refocus our attention on that unity. "Triduum" (pronounced TRID-oo-um) is a Latin term meaning quite simply "three days." It is a thoroughly "churchy" word, not to be found even in most unabridged dictionaries until very recently.[6] What is important is not that the word be introduced to churchgoers but that the reality of a unified observance spread across three days be evident to those who attend the rites of the Triduum.

One way of making clear the unity of the separated observances is this: Have no benediction at the close of the Thursday and Friday services, but announce or enter a notation in the Thursday bulletin thus: "Our service continues tomorrow at [hour]." In the Friday bulletin, note: "Our service, begun yesterday evening, will conclude with the Great Vigil of Easter at [hour]." Given the solemnity of Thursday and Friday, often it is also suggested that worshipers depart from these occasions in silence. Practices that normally signal the beginning of the service (organ voluntary, responsive greeting, opening collect) can be deleted at the Friday service and at the Vigil.

Thus there is but one opening act (on Thursday evening) and one closing act (at the culmination of the Vigil).

But form points to meaning, not to itself. The meaning is that the passion, death, and resurrection of the Lord is one divine action, separated in time by us—partly for the sake of convenience, but primarily to allow space for the contemplation and assimilation demanded by so great a mystery as this:

> Ah, holy Jesus, how hast thou offended,
> that we to judge thee have in hate pretended?
> By foes derided, by thine own rejected, O most afflicted!
>
> Who was the guilty? Who brought this upon thee?
> Alas, my treason, Jesus, hath undone thee!
> 'Twas I, Lord Jesus, I it was denied thee; I crucified thee.
>
> Lo, the Good Shepherd for the sheep is offered;
> the slave hath sinned, and the Son hath suffered.
> For our atonement, while we nothing heeded, God interceded.[7]

That the very anointed One of God should die and rise on behalf of us who willfully cried "Crucify!" is a thing at which we must marvel slowly, not something we glance at for an instant.

Holy Thursday

Within contemporary rites for Holy Thursday evening, three actions predominate: footwashing, the Eucharist, and the stripping of the altar.[8] Before examining these in detail, two other matters sometimes connected with this occasion should be discussed.

First, out of a well-intended desire to understand our Jewish roots, it has sometimes become popular to have the Eucharist preceded by (or even incorporated into) some adaptation of the Seder, the meal that characterizes the Passover. This is not to be encouraged for several reasons. (a) The Seder as it is used today has evolved over centuries and now includes practices utterly unknown in the time of Jesus; hence, we cannot really do what Jesus did. (b) Because of the differing chronologies of the Synoptics and John, and of various other historical issues, it is not certain that a Seder was observed on the evening before the crucifixion. (c) A "Jewish meal" presided over by

92

Christians who will inevitably impose upon it connotations not inherent to it is suspect as to integrity at best; at worst this may produce a very distorted understanding of the relationship between Judaism and Christianity. Devout Jews often take offense at the spectacle of Christians who want to "play at being Jewish" one evening a year. If this seems strange, we might well ask how we would feel about Muslims periodically having a kind of baptismal or eucharistic rite in order to try to "get in touch with their Christian roots." Christians who wish to participate authentically in a Seder are well advised not to attempt to combine this with the Holy Thursday Eucharist but rather to inquire whether they might be invited to participate in the family Seder in the household of Jewish friends.

A second practice that has become popular in recent decades is the service of Tenebrae, held on either the evening of Holy Thursday or of Good Friday, or both. "Tenebrae" means darkness or gloom and has its origins in a complex monastic liturgy of the Middle Ages. There, fifteen candles were extinguished one by one across Wednesday, Thursday, and Friday evenings as a part of the traditional monastic offices. Recent adaptations share little with the medieval tradition except for the use of candles. Because now the rite is done over two evenings, or on only one, and because we find the allegorical interpretation of the Hebrew Scriptures during Holy Week more mystifying than edifying, recent Tenebrae rites are quite varied and sometimes of questionable content and value. One of the better adaptations uses sixteen segments of St. John's passion in contemporary translation on Good Friday evening.[9] Before any such service is attempted, very careful preparation must be made. Rehearsals should be held under the lighting conditions of the actual service; too many of these services have been rehearsed in daylight with no attention given to how much illumination is needed for the later readings or how readers will move about in a darkened chancel. As a result a service that requires great dignity and decorum has been destroyed.

Now concerning the more fully established practices for Holy Thursday: The footwashing is related to the Gospel for this occasion, John 13:1-17, 31b-35. In some places only a few preselected persons join in the action, but in others all present are invited to participate.

The service requires careful preparation and interpretation; the act of washing should be voluntary, so that those who prefer not to take part will feel that without discomfort they can attend in order to participate fully in other portions of the evening's rites. Those who find footwashing a strange innovation ("too Catholic," they may well say) may be helped by the reminder that it has long been a consistent practice among groups such as the Brethren and Seventh Day Adventists.

During the initial recovery of the footwashing practice by other Protestants, there was much discussion about cultural relevance. We do not commonly walk dusty roads in sandals; and upon arriving for a dinner party, those who are hosting it do not provide a servant with a basin of water and towel. So is this a custom so unconnected to our culture as to be artificial? Is there some way of "updating" the act so it does connect with us? (Shining another person's shoes was suggested, or washing hands rather than feet. Neither worked well—the latter in particular because it was too reminiscent on this evening of the action of Pontius Pilate.)

While rites disconnected from daily experience are a matter of legitimate liturgical concern, in this instance the very strangeness of the act may reinforce its significance. In doing the task of a household servant, Jesus is giving us an example of humble service. To do something a bit strange, embarrassing even, is more likely to be an experience in humility than to do something quite familiar. But of greater importance: In this act we are remembering Jesus in that usual Hebraic way, by reenacting a past event in order that it may become our present experience—anamnesis. Footwashing can be a compressed means of recalling the full extent of divine humiliation from manger to cross, and thus is a way of binding together on this evening all that we need to have in heart and mind as we begin to keep the Triduum.

The eucharistic aspect of Holy Thursday has been generally retained even by groups of Christians who have abandoned all else on this evening. But in those very circles, the rite whose ancient name means "thanksgiving" has tended to be an occasion for deep sadness or even morbidity. Because of the approaching denial, desertion, and crucifixion of Jesus, Holy Thursday evening has its inescapably solemn motifs; but these are best expressed in the later action of the stripping of the altar. Indeed the best reason for restoring that custom where it has been lost is thereby to allow the Eucharist to have joyful rather than mournful meaning.

But how can Jesus' last meal with the disciples be joyful? Remember that we must read the sacred story backward. We cannot even pretend to forget momentarily that this is not Jesus' last meal.[10] The great, final meal of the followers of Jesus with their Lord will be the festive banquet of heaven. Between the supper in the upper room and that great feast lie the meals of the resurrection appearances, which (a) reinterpret the Holy Thursday supper and (b) anticipate in our experience the heavenly festival. What happened at Emmaus, and in Jerusalem when Jesus ate in the presence of the astonished disciples, and at Galilee where the Risen One prepared breakfast for them—all of this makes new the meaning of the Holy Thursday evening meal. This Thursday's Eucharist is a supreme instance of a refreshing table prepared in the midst of enemies and of the fusion of anamnesis and prolepsis in our experience.

On all other occasions, through the instrument of the Eucharist, we give thanks to God for a wide variety of things: for particular events in the story of Jesus as commemorated in the liturgical calendar, for the joy of a wedding or an ordination or the consecration of a new building, for the promise of eternal life on the day of a funeral; the list is virtually without end. On all other occasions, we give thanks for particular gifts through the Eucharist. But on this occasion we give thanks for the gift of the Eucharist itself. We praise God for taking what might have been nothing more than a sad farewell of teacher and disciples and transforming it into a way of revealing the presence of the Risen One. We praise God for turning an occasion for deep mourning into an occasion of profound gratitude. On Holy Thursday the church lifts up the fist of faith and shakes it defiantly at every potential evildoer, saying, "We have this meal to strengthen and sustain us. It is the reliable promise of divine power and presence always in our midst. We will fear no evil, because our God submits to no destroyer, not even death. Thanks be to God for the gift of this meal!" Only when we have shouted defiantly at the hosts of evil are we ready to confront them more directly; and so the Holy Thursday service proceeds to recall the passion of the Lord and thus to prepare for Friday.

The stripping of the altar at the close of the Thursday rite operates at two levels. Symbolically it conveys the humiliation of Jesus as his clothes are taken from him. Psychologically it makes as bare as possible the worship space and thus sets up a powerful visual contrast for the rest of the Triduum. On Good Friday there will be no flowers, no lighted candles, no colorful paraments or vestments. Items that cannot be removed may well be "veiled," covered over with black fabric so that only their outlines can be discerned. But then on Easter the same space will abound with an array of flowers and candles; the best paraments and vestments will be used. Although these cannot represent the resurrection itself (which is far beyond human expression in any form), they will connote our sorrow turned to joy, divine humiliation transmuted to exaltation.

Good Friday

In current practice Good Friday can be something other than what has commonly characterized services on this day. Although Catholics and Protestants in the past have followed somewhat different forms, in both camps the observances have been such as to cause people to ask, "Then why do we call this Friday 'good'?" Emphasis has been on the seemingly senseless human suffering of Jesus rather than on the purposeful humiliation of God through which redemption comes. In other words, we have failed once again to read the sacred story backward. Friday has been observed as if Sunday had never come.

Good Friday should and can proclaim divine purpose as paramount. Indeed, the term "Good Friday" may be a corruption of the English phrase "God's Friday." And this day is good precisely because God was in control at Calvary. The crucifixion of Jesus was not some bad deal that God had to try to make the best of; it was a working out of divine intention with a view to the salvation of an otherwise doomed creation.

It is not insignificant that the passion narratives of Matthew, Mark, and Luke rotate across the three lectionary years for use on Palm-Passion Sunday, but that always on Good Friday John's narrative is to be read. The import of this is lost on us, in large part because of a relatively recent scissors-and-paste version of the passion known as "the seven last words of Jesus," in which the four

Gospel accounts are cut apart and put back together in ways that would undoubtedly perplex the four Evangelists. So before understanding Good Friday, we must review some basics of biblical interpretation.

Because Christianity is a historical faith that relies greatly upon the process of God's activity across time, the historical development of the New Testament is not an optional consideration. Although there has been some debate as to whether Mark was written before Matthew, the general consensus is that it was; and there is no debate that these two books preceded the Third and Fourth Gospels. In both Mark and Matthew, Jesus is reported to have said only one thing from the cross: "My God, my God, why have you forsaken me?" Well-meaning interpreters have tried to blunt this cry by suggesting Jesus was merely (in good pious Jewish fashion) quoting from the psalms, and that in order to understand the meaning we must read Psalm 22 through to its glorious conclusion. But that is to ignore both other data in these two Gospels and the historical situation from which they arose.

As Paul indicated (before any of the Gospels were written), the cross is seen by those outside the faith as a scandal and foolishness (1 Cor. 1:18-25). By using it so profusely as a decoration in our churches and as jewelry on our persons, we have domesticated the cross to the point of forgetting that in its original setting it was the instrument of execution for those guilty of heinous crimes. The earliest Christians, in contrast, agonizingly wrestled with how to react to the ignominy of serving One who had been executed as a criminal. Thus in the earliest Gospels, the cross reflects this agony and projects it onto God. The whole creation is in agony along with the Creator: The sky grows black at midday, the earth is convulsed so that even the dead are rousted out of their graves. God is in agony for the sin of creation.

Without denying or diminishing any of that, Luke (who writes a bit later) expounds the purpose of this agony. In Luke's Gospel, Jesus says only three things from the cross; two of them explicitly point to God's redemptive purpose: "Father, forgive them; for they do not know what they are doing" and "Truly I tell you, today you will be with me in Paradise." There is both general amnesty for unintentional sin and particular amnesty for deliberate transgression. Finally Jesus says, "Father, into your hands I commend my spirit." This seals Luke's assertion that the cross is not some curveball thrown at God; divine agony is consonant with divine purpose, and therefore God can be trusted for the results.

Then comes John, whose Gospel is read on Good Friday. He writes still later, with the benefit of further contemplation by the church on the meaning of the cross. Thus John finds still deeper significance that complements without contradicting the insights of the earlier writers. John's particular assertion is this: The purposeful agony of God is not a short-term matter (how God responded on the spot when Jesus was sentenced to death) but nothing less than the long-term work of grace. In other words, God is in control at the cross, not as one who reacts to events but as the One who directs their course. Consider several aspects of this direction, reported only by John:

1) In Gethsemane, when Jesus says, "I am the one you are seeking," the Roman arrest party falls to the ground stunned. But instead of running to escape, Jesus (with seeming impatience) retorts, "I told you, I am the one you are looking for." In other words, Jesus, not the Roman soldiers, is in charge of the proceedings and is determined to move them forward.

2) Before Pilate, Jesus says with great determination: "You would have no power over me unless it had been given from above." Here is as explicit a statement of John's assertion as could be made. Later Pilate implicitly assents to divine control by refusing to reword the placard declaring "Jesus of Nazareth, the King of the Jews."

3) In John Jesus says only three things from the cross, all without parallel in the Synoptics, and each is a word of control. (a) "Woman, here is your son. . . . Here is your mother." Jesus will not turn over the care of Mary to custom, let alone chance. Jesus controls her custody, contrary to usual practices that a widowed mother will be cared for by family members. (b) "I am thirsty" is not merely a word about dehydration. John specifically says this is uttered "to fulfill the scripture"—a formula he employs at four other places in his passion account (13:18, 17:12, 19:24, and 19:36-37). (c) "It is finished" is an anemic rendering of the Greek verb *tetelestai,* which implies the transmission of something from afar (the same *tele* as in telephone,

telegraph, and television). "It is finished" does not mean "It's all over now" but means "That which has been far off is now brought near; the goal is accomplished." In other words, the eternal purpose of God is now achieved.

4) Death by crucifixion results not from loss of blood but from suffocation, and the process can last days if the legs of the crucified are strong and thus capable of supporting the body. Hence John reports that the soldiers come to break the legs of those who were crucified, and thus to hasten death so that they will not be on the cross for the Passover, which would be an offense to the devout. But Jesus is already dead. How is that again? Is not this a carpenter, presumably with strong legs, and a man of only thirty years? How can he be dead so soon? The answer is found much farther back in the Gospel when Jesus says: "I lay down my life in order to take it up again. No one takes it from me, but I lay it down of my own accord. I have power to lay it down, and I have power to take it up again. I have received this command from my Father" (10:17b-18). Lest there be any doubt, God is in charge here.

Thus again and again the Fourth Gospel presses the point: The forgiving agony of God fulfills the divine and eternal purpose of redemption. That is why this is both God's Friday and Good Friday. That is also why on this day the faithful gather less to contemplate the pain of a dying man than to rejoice in the purposes of a Creator who willingly suffers for the creature.

But all of that is lost when we produce "seven words from the cross" by ignoring historical development and turning to scissors and paste. So what should occur? If we are the people of God called and disciplined to carry on the work of Christ in the power of the Spirit, then on this day we are chiefly to do what the Savior did upon the cross: To offer ourselves for the world, and that particularly by way of intercession. (Let it be clear that we are not co-atoners with the Savior. We do not create the Good News, but we are entrusted with the task of conveying it to others.)

Far from being an introverted occasion on which I consider primarily what Jesus did for me on the cross, Good Friday should be an extroverted occasion on which we as church consider how best we can present to the world the redemption of God, both by word and by deed. Among other things, this means that Good Friday is the premier occasion for intercession; on this day the church prays for the entire creation for which Christ died. There are no exclusions because the divine love revealed at Calvary knows no bounds. One corollary possibility is for congregations (preferably cooperatively and ecumenically) to hold a prayer vigil from the close of the Good Friday portion of the Triduum to the beginning of the Great Vigil. This can be accompanied by the traditional pre-Easter fast.

Increasingly by virtue of work schedules, the old three-hour service of devotion on Friday afternoon is evolving into a shorter Friday evening service. This is in itself an honorable way of scrapping the "seven last words" pattern. But where a longer format is to be retained, a service might be constructed around "three views of the crucified One," as indicated above in the consideration of the Gospel passion narratives, with ample time for intercessions.

A Lenten devotion that became popular primarily as a private practice arose in the fifteenth century. After a number of variations were sorted out, this "Stations of the Cross" service settled into the contemplation of fourteen events—eight based on Gospel material (but again assembled by the scissors-and-paste method), and six rooted in later tradition. Adaptations of this service are best used at some time other than during the congregational service on Good Friday.

Traditionally there has been no celebration of the Eucharist at all on Holy Saturday; and if communion is distributed on Good Friday, it is done with bread and wine remaining from the Thursday evening service without a eucharistic prayer over newly presented elements. In Roman Catholic tradition primarily, eucharistic bread, normally kept in a special receptacle, called the "tabernacle," is moved to a different location at the close of the Thursday service for use in private devotion; on Friday and Saturday the door of the tabernacle stands open to reveal its emptiness.

The Great Vigil of Easter

We come now to the final segment of the Triduum, by means of which the Great Fifty Days are inaugurated. The service begins at dusk on Saturday, at the earliest, but is more effective when it commences before daybreak on Sunday; thus, the congregation enters the church in darkness and leaves (after two or three hours) in full daylight. By its design the Vigil recapitulates Lenten themes as it provides the final transition into Easter. Thus, it is best appreciated by those who have attended regularly throughout Lent. Those who attend services only once or twice a year will understandably be mystified by what occurs at the Vigil, and probably will be greatly annoyed by its physical duration and liturgical comprehensiveness. The Vigil is not for the faint of heart!

Denominational rites are available and vary only slightly.[11] Always the Great Vigil consists of four parts: (1) Service of Light, (2) Service of the Word, (3) Baptism and Reaffirmation, (4) Eucharist. Now we expand briefly on each portion.

1) The service begins in virtual darkness. If weather does not permit the congregation to gather outside, the service best begins in a location apart from the worship space (such as a social hall). As the service begins, a fire is kindled in token of Christ the Sun of Justice rising from death endowed with healing power. From the fire the great Paschal Candle is lighted and carried at the head of a procession.[12] This is the largest candle ever used by the church. It is reminiscent of the pillar of fire in the wilderness: Christ is our liberator and guide who leads us out of sin and death's captivity, even as Moses led the people through the sea. From the great candle, individual candles carried in procession by the worshipers are lighted. When the candle is placed in its stand, an ancient hymn ("The Exsultet") is sung. Its words bespeak the mystery of the shared flame, divided yet undimmed, and call upon all on earth and in heaven to praise the Risen Lord of Life.

2) The Service of the Word provides for readings concerning creation, the deluge, Abraham's offering of Isaac, Israel's deliverance at the sea, God's renewal of Israel, the divine offer of salvation to all, the promise of the covenant within our hearts, Ezekiel's vision of the dry bones, and the restoration of Israel after the Exile. When used in its entirety (and always at least the Exodus account must be included), the full scope of the sacred history of the first creation is set forth, and the major themes of Lent are recapitulated. Then the new creation in Christ is joyfully announced by the reading of Romans 6:3-11 and of the Gospel account of the resurrection provided in that lectionary year. (In some forms of the Vigil, baptism is

101

interposed between the Old and New Testament readings; in other forms all of the readings and sermon precede baptism—the pattern set forth here.) Until the reading of the Gospel, the building may be lighted only dimly. Then the church is fully illuminated, revealing its Easter array of flowers and furnishings. It is appropriate, however, for this portion of the service to be the reversal of the stripping of the altar on Thursday evening. Instead of being arrayed in advance, as a part of the liturgy the chancel can now be vested for Easter.[13]

3) It is highly desirable that baptisms actually occur during the third section of the Great Vigil. This was in the ancient church the primary—indeed at points almost the exclusive—occasion for baptism; for regardless of how it is administered, baptism is always our incorporation into the death and resurrection of the Lord.[14] Whether or not it is possible to carry out an actual baptism, always the congregation reaffirms its baptismal commitment—an experience for which Lent has been a six-and-a-half-week preparation. Most recent denominational rites of baptism provide forms by which such congregational reaffirmation can be effected.

4) The most joyful Eucharist of the liturgical year concludes the Great Vigil. For those who have kept an actual fast in preparation, this is the great "break-fast" prepared by the Risen One, who made a morning meal for his followers at the seashore as a way of revealing himself to them (John 21:9-14). For all communicants it is the recognition of their Lord in the breaking of the bread. After the extended journey of the Forty Days, the Great Fifty Days have begun with intense joy:

> At the Lamb's high banquet called to share,
> arrayed in garments white and fair,
> the Red Sea past, we now would sing
> to Jesus, our triumphant king.
>
> Protected in the Paschal night
> from the destroying angel's might,
> in triumph went the ransomed free
> from Pharaoh's cruel tyranny.
> Now Christ our Passover is slain,
> the Lamb of God without a stain;

his flesh, the true unleavened bread,
is freely offered in our stead.

O all-sufficient Sacrifice,
beneath thee hell defeated lies;
thy captive people are set free,
and endless life restored in thee.[15]

5

Christmas: The Great Exchange

Christmas is the season of the great exchange. Greeting cards are exchanged, as are social invitations and visits. Gifts are exchanged around the Christmas tree on December 25—and at store counters on December 26. But none of that begins to approximate what is meant here by "the great exchange." For in the depths of its meaning Christmas is about the exchange of divinity and humanity, of eternity and temporality, of life and death.

The season's familiarity and its immense popular appeal obscure the fact that Christmas is a mystery comparable to that of the Pasch and fully dependent on faith in the Paschal victory. The wonder of Christmas is not, as might be supposed, "How can a virgin bear a child?" The virginal conception of Jesus is not in itself the mystery but is rather one way of pointing to the mystery, of indicating that what occurred at Bethlehem is outside the bounds of both human experience and explanation. The marvel is that the creator of the cosmos comes as creature for the purpose of setting right all that has gone wrong on this tiny planet. The wonder is that the Eternal One who can be neither created nor destroyed willingly becomes subject both to birth and to death.

At work here again is the conviction that all of this can be perceived only from our side of the cross. No one during the ministry of Jesus seemed to have the slightest suspicion that this Galilean teacher was anything other than one of us. When Jesus began to teach in Nazareth, the townspeople were astounded:

> They said, "Where did this man get all this? What is this wisdom that has been given to him? What deeds of power are being done by his hands! Is not this the carpenter, the son of Mary and brother of James and Joses and Judas and Simon, and are not his sisters here with us?" And they took offense at him. (Mark 6:2-3)

Even the bold confession of Peter at Caesarea Philippi, "You are the messiah," if considered at the level of historical event (rather than later interpretation of that event) should not be read as implying divine origin; messiah was expected to be God's anointed one, but still a human leader. Messiah would be some person God would choose and appoint; that this person would be the very incarnation of the Eternal was beyond imagining.

But confronted with the crucifixion and resurrection of Jesus (and its essential difference from the death and resuscitation of Lazarus or Jairus' daughter), the church before long had to ask: "Is this inaugurator of a new creation simply one of us, as limited as we are in time, in space, in obedience to God?" The answer kept coming back, "No! This is One sent from God in a way that we have never known before. For the new creation cannot be inaugurated except by the One who fashioned the creation in the first place. This One is fully obedient and freed from the constraints of time and space." After the Synoptic writers have begun this process of reinterpretation about who Jesus is, then comes the Gospel of John, which opens not with a birth narrative (as do Matthew and Luke) but with a profound theological assertion reaching back even beyond creation itself:

> In the beginning was the Word, and the Word was with God, and the Word was God. He was in the beginning with God. All things came into being through him, and without him not one thing came into being. What has come into being in him was life, and the life was the light of all people. . . . And the Word became flesh and lived among us, and we have seen his glory, the glory as of a father's only son, full of grace and truth. (John 1:1-4, 14)

Christmas commemorates the appearing of that Eternal Word in our midst. To settle for the romance of a displaced mother giving birth in a stable, to argue about how a virgin can conceive a child, is to bring profundity to the brink of ruin. Christmas is the enfleshment of God, the humiliation of the Most High and divine participation in all that is painful, ugly, frustrating, and limited. Divinity takes on humanity, to restore the image of God implanted at creation but sullied by sin. Here is the great exchange Christmas ponders, that God became like us that we might become like God. God accepted death that the world might accept life. The Creator assumed temporality to redeem creation from futility. A hymn writer summarizes it this way:

> This night of wonder, night of joy,
> was born the Christ, our brother;
> he comes, not mighty to destroy,
> to bid us love each other.
> How could he quit his kingly state
> for such a world of greed and hate?
> What deep humiliation
> secured the world's salvation![1]

The Twelve Days of Christmas

"On the first day of Christmas my true love gave to me a partridge in a pear tree" is more than a frivolous holiday diversion.[2] It is the evidence that once Christmas truly was celebrated as a season of twelve days—not simply a day, and not December 25 plus however many preceding days might be needed to make preparations for it. Particularly in "merry old England" the entire twelve days were filled with celebration, often in the nature of secular revelry, which was one of the things to which the Puritans objected so strenuously. Indeed on the west side of the Atlantic, where the Puritans got their way, it was at times illegal to take off work on December 25 or to commemorate the Lord's birth in any outward way. Christmas observances were deemed idolatrous, or at least considered undesirable remnants of Roman Catholicism. (It did not elude the Puritans that "Christmas" is simply a contraction of "Christ's Mass" in reference to the festival Eucharist on this occasion in the Roman Church.)[3]

We find it difficult to believe, but the universal recovery of the observance of Christmas by Protestants in the United States came only after great controversy in many quarters; in Massachusetts, where Christmas had been specifically outlawed from 1659 to 1681, December 25 did not become a legal holiday until 1856. For the most part, what got recovered once we did make our peace with Christmas festivities was Christmas Day without the other eleven days.[4] In one of those ironies history seems to love, we have now developed a "Christmas season" that begins before December 25 and extends backward to early December (or November, or even September in the commercial world) instead of extending forward for twelve days.

Should we try to buck cultural forces in an attempt to reverse the process? Yes and no. On the one hand, until the recent process of lectionary revision, the careful observance of Advent was necessary to stress the future dimension of history. For any affirmation of Christ's final reign of justice has been largely lost in popular piety's usual interpretations of Christmas. (If you doubt this, go through your Christmas cards and see how many, instead of wishing you a happy new year, extend wishes for justice and transformation at the end of time.) Until recently, holding the line on when to begin Christmas had great importance as a means of preserving the Christian insistence that the resurrection is primarily about the future.

In the revised lectionary system, however, not only is Advent preceded by the Sunday that celebrates Christ's reign in glory, but the earlier Sundays in November also have themes about the end of time and the judgment. In a sense, we have accommodated culture by backing up the calendar rather than to risk irritating people who are in a "christmasy" mood by telling them in mid-December, "You can't celebrate Christmas yet." What used to be the theme of Advent almost exclusively, is now well considered even before Advent begins. So if the themes once reserved for Advent now back up into early November, it may be less lamentable that the themes of Christmas back up into mid-December. The Christian calendar, after all, not only has an evolutionary history; its evolution continues in our midst. But great integrity must be maintained to ensure that the eschatological texts will be taken seriously in November if Christmas is going to be allowed to back up into late Advent.

Some congregations effect a compromise between historical liturgical categories and cultural realities by distinguishing clearly (without necessarily articulating this well) between what can happen during congregational worship and what is permissible at other times. Thus narratives about the nativity are not read nor are familiar carols sung in worship until Christmas Eve; but such activities can be included in a children's pageant on a Saturday afternoon during Advent or at the meeting of a church society on December 10.

On the other hand, good arguments can be set forth for holding the old demarcations between Advent and Christmas, and for keeping Christmas as a full season that begins at sunset on December 24. One of the functions of the church in any age is to stand over against the prevailing culture. Often people sense this in ways that come out in oblique comments: "Isn't it a pity that we are too busy at Christmas time to remember what it is really all about?" But all of that busyness stops on December 26. There are yet ten or eleven days in which to "remember what it is really all about." Suppose the church alleviated some of the pre–Christmas Day pressure by scheduling its Christmas parties and pageants between December 26 and January 6. Suppose that those churches which have usually halted the observance of Christmas on December 25 kept its emphases on the Sundays following. Why should the church stop singing carols simply because the department stores have shifted back to playing secular selections over their public address systems?

The observances of Christmas Eve and Day usually are clearly established by local custom and need little elaboration here as to form. Christmas Eve services are rather standard for Protestants; many of these are eucharistic in nature, and quite appropriately so.[5] For as once at Bethlehem God came among us in the humble guise of what seemed to be an ordinary baby, so still God comes to us in humble guises; and the presence of Christ proclaimed in bread and wine is not only one of these guises but is also a clue to how we are to discover this Christ in our midst in all kinds of other seemingly ordinary circumstances. Further, the Eucharist is always a means of thanksgiving; and the great exchange of divinity and humanity should be a perpetual source of grateful rejoicing.

Some Christmas Eve services incorporate the lighting of candles; this practice is theologically derivative of the passing of the light from the Paschal Candle at Easter, but there are remnants also of the rationale often given for placing Christmas near the end of December. No one knows when Jesus was born. When the observance of the nativity began to be kept liturgically in the fourth century, it came to be inserted into the calendar at the place where northern hemisphere peoples since ancient times had celebrated "the return of the invincible sun," as the shortest day of the year passed and the days began to lengthen. This placement had a practical benefit in giving converts from solar cults something cultic to do at the old, accustomed time. (The church has always been good at adapting its practices to displace what it deems to be less desirable ones.) A theological justification was not difficult to find: Christ, not the sun in the heavens, is our true light. In the nativity we mark the particular coming of this light into the world (related to John 1:4-9). When candles are lighted by worshipers at the close of the Christmas Eve service and then carried out by them, this act is a reminder of our charge to let our light shine before others and to carry the Good News of Christ into the world (Matt. 5:16).

Regardless of what else happens liturgically at Christmas, always there are carols. For the record: From the standpoint of professional musicians, "carol" is a technical term limited to a certain style of music that originated as a circular dance (from the Middle English word *carole*, meaning ring or circle); carol tunes can support any kind of content and are by no means limited to Christmas, or even to religious practice. Purists on this issue will distinguish between Christmas carols ("Infant Holy, Infant Lowly" and "Sing We Now of Christmas") and Christmas hymns ("O Come, All Ye Faithful" and "Hark! the Herald Angels Sing"). But such distinctions are lost on most people; "carol" has come to be popularly defined as words appropriate at Christmas, regardless of the musical form to which they are sung. And the term "Easter carol" seems to these same people to be an oxymoron. It is not a battle worth fighting. I set it down, as I have said, "just for the record." Often whole services of worship are built around scripture readings and carols; one such "lessons and carols" pattern is derived from a service that has been popularized in our time at the chapel of King's College, Cambridge, England, and is widely copied and adapted.[6]

Also popular at this time of year are choir presentations, such as *A Ceremony of Carols* by Benjamin Britten, or appropriate parts of Handel's oratorio *Messiah*. It is a pity that so often in churches (as distinct from what may be fitting in concert halls) these are regarded as pieces to be performed for an audience rather than as integral parts of participatory congregational worship. With a little effort such works can be set in the context of prayers, scripture readings, and even a sermon and well-chosen carol or two, so that the choir assists in leading the worship of the people instead of giving a musical concert more for the enjoyment than for the mutual edification of all present. Much can be learned in this regard by studying Bach's *Christmas Oratorio,* which is actually six cantatas, each for a specific day's liturgy (December 25, 26, 27, the Circumcision, the Sunday immediately following, and the Epiphany). As is characteristic of Bach cantatas, these were built around familiar chorale tunes, so congregational singing within the cantata was expected.

Whatever services are traditional at Christmas, or are introduced, most careful consideration should be given to content that plumbs the depths of the New Testament proclamation about the nativity of Jesus. Only in this way will we move beyond a preoccupation with a sweet baby in a crib (or Santa Claus) to ask the basic question: "Who is this that was born in Bethlehem and is headed toward death in Jerusalem?"[7]

The Epiphany and Beyond

It is this very issue of identity that the Epiphany has come to signify. Among Roman Catholics and Protestants, the Epiphany (that is, "the manifestation" or "the appearance") has for centuries been observed on January 6 at the close of the Twelve Days. Its observance had primarily to do with the arrival of the Magi. In the Eastern churches, on the other hand, January 6 has come to be celebrated primarily as the baptism of Jesus and his first miracle at Cana.[8]

In recent decades several factors have combined to alter actual practice in the West. (1) It is no longer practical to have a large celebration on January 6 when this date falls on a weekday. (2) Popular piety has collapsed into one event Luke's account of the arrival of the shepherds at the stable after hearing an angelic announcement and Matthew's report of the arrival of the Magi at a house after seeing a star. In contrast to earlier depictions, which kept these separated, modern crèches and Christmas illustrations show everyone together at a manger. Indeed, we take this quite for granted until in vain we search art museum walls hunting a painting that shows shepherds and Magi together. (3) The West has seen great wisdom in the Eastern emphasis on the Baptism of the Lord at this season, in contrast to the basic liturgical neglect of the baptism in the

West except as related to the temptation of Jesus at the beginning of Lent.

Therefore in recent decades many Western churches have altered the historical calendar as follows: The Baptism of the Lord is to be commemorated on the Sunday following January 6 (anytime from January 7 to 13). Except when January 6 falls on Sunday, the arrival of the Magi is to be commemorated on the Sunday prior to January 6.[9]

But what common thread is there between Christmas Day, the Epiphany, and the Baptism of the Lord? Summed up in one word: Identification. The coming of the Magi and the Baptism of Jesus help us to identify who it is that is born in Bethlehem and thus enable us to get past "the cute baby" approach that so vitiates the deep meaning of the incarnation and prevents us from appreciating the great exchange of divinity and humanity.

The identification of the newborn as recorded in Luke's Gospel (and read on Christmas Eve and Day) is mediated by angels to shepherds. Contrary to our romantic notions based on Psalm 23, in the first century shepherds were regarded with suspicion, even despised, among the settled peoples of Judea. Because they were generally poor and nomadic, shepherds were feared as a kind of wandering, potentially criminal element in the land. To these, not to the noble or the elite, God sent heavenly messengers with good tidings. And the shepherds were the first in Luke's Gospel to have unquestioning faith. When aged Zechariah was confronted by Gabriel, he raised questions about the plausibility of the angelic message; Mary later questioned the angel about the manner in which the promise to her could be fulfilled. But the shepherds asked no questions. They went to Bethlehem "with haste"; and they "returned, glorifying and praising God" and bearing witness to all they had seen and heard (Luke 2:16-20). Thus Jesus is identified as the One who is made known to the outcasts, who elicits faith from the despised of the world in fulfillment of the words of Mary's song (Luke 1:46-55).

The coming of the Magi is complementary in meaning to the adoration of the shepherds. In contrast to the lowly of Judea, the Magi are Gentiles, the high and mighty from afar; they need no angelic chorus, for they have the ability to discern the movements of the stars and the planets. They do need the guidance of the Hebrew Scriptures, which is given to them a bit unwittingly at Herod's court—where shepherds certainly would never have been admitted, let alone given counsel.

Tradition amplifies what Matthew's Gospel lacks. Ultimately the number of the Magi settled down to three. Once it was believed there were twelve, to correspond to the twelve tribes of Israel. (Usually we fail to note that Matthew specifies three kinds of gifts, but not the number of gift-bearers.) Working from traditions that amplified the story of the Magi, artists depicted them to be of various ages and ethnic groups: one elderly, one middle-aged, one young; one black, sometimes two white, but often one Caucasian and one Mongol. Although these details have no basis in Matthew's narrative, they are consistent with the Gospel's intention of identifying Jesus as a messiah for all people.

What Matthew does specify, and undoubtedly intends to be interpreted according to the usual symbolism of that day, is the three types of gifts presented. Gold was the prerogative of monarchs, who commonly owned all of it they could get their hands on. Incense was used in many ancient cultures in religious rites to indicate the presence of the deity.[10] Myrrh was used as a painkiller (Mark 15:23), an embalming substance (John 19:39), a fragrance (Ps. 45:8), and a beauty treatment (Esther 2:12); it was added to the oil used when anointing priests (Exod. 30:23). Thus by the gifts they bring, the Magi identify Jesus as the supreme ruler of the world; as God's anointed (= messiah) high priest; and as the suffering servant who dies as a fragrant and beautiful offering before God.[11]

The baptismal narratives also identify who Jesus is, both overtly and subtly. The overt identification is in the voice from heaven that says to Jesus: "You are my Son, the Beloved; with you I am well pleased" (Mark 1:11 = Luke 3:22. Cf. Matt. 3:17 in which the statement is made to the bystanders about Jesus). Also quite overt as to Jesus' identity are the Johannine declarations about the baptized One: "Here is the Lamb of God who takes away the sin of the world"; " 'He . . . is the one who baptizes with the Holy Spirit.' And I [John the baptizer] myself have seen and have testified that this is the Son of God" (John 1:29, 33-34).[12]

113

The much more subtle identifications of Jesus in the Synoptic accounts of the baptism are worth at least equal consideration, particularly since our lack of familiarity with the Hebrew Scriptures prevents us from recognizing them. Note that in the baptismal accounts there is mention of water, movement like unto that of a dove, and the sound of a voice. These are the motifs of Genesis 1:1, where the spirit of God hovers over the waters and the voice of God says, "Let there be light." So? So Jesus is identified here as the One who is inaugurating the new creation. The One who is baptized as if he were a common sinner in need of repentance is, in fact, the architect of the universe, come to redeem what has gone awry. The great exchange, again! But water, the dove or the movement of air, and voice of God are also reminiscent of two other crucial pentateuchal stories: that of the great Flood and that of the Exodus. For Jesus is both the New Noah, come to deliver the world from sin and institute the covenant of grace under the sign of the rainbow, and the New Moses, come to open the way into the life of freedom from bondage.[13]

Where the story of the wedding at Cana is used at this season, it bears yet one more mark of identification: Jesus is the One whose ministry is to be characterized by wonders. But these wonders were not, like those of the magicians of the day, intended merely to astound or amuse the observer. These wonders were to be seen as signs—reliable indicators that God was authentically at work in Jesus, so that the glory of God would be revealed and received by faith. (See John 2:11.)

Dependent Observances

Five observances depend on Christmas for both their placement and their meaning; of these, four lie outside the Christmas season: the Annunciation on March 25, the Visitation on May 31, the Birth of John the Baptizer on June 24, and the Presentation of Jesus on February 2. The observance within the Christmas season is the Circumcision or Name of Jesus on January 1.

Despite the fact that all of these commemorations arise from the chronology of Luke's birth and infancy narrative, many free church Protestants have never observed any of them; in one of the ironies of life, the more loudly congregations proclaim that they have "biblical worship" or "New Testament worship" (whatever those terms may mean) the less likely they are to pay any attention to these events recorded in the Third Gospel. Observing the occasions does present certain difficulties, but these are not insurmountable. A primary difficulty is that of being unable to sustain weekday worship. In churches without calendars that have fixed rules of precedence, consideration can be given to observing these occasions on the nearest Lord's Day, since, after all, they are events related to the life of Jesus.

The actual chief impediment in many places is a revulsion against the observances due to the place they have had in the Roman Catholic and Orthodox churches; this, for the most part, is irrational since it is based on grave misconceptions about the teachings of those churches and even on gross unfamiliarity with anything in the first two chapters of Luke's Gospel except for the account of the nativity itself (2:1-20). Observance of the dependent events reveals the fuller Lucan story (with strains of Matthew 1:18-24 echoing in the events of annunciation and naming) and, in four of the five instances, encourages the church to reflect on the meaning of the Great Exchange at times outside the Christmas season.

Annunciation

Placed exactly nine months ahead of the nativity, this observance (based on Luke 1:26-38) falls within Lent, except in the occasional year when it collides with Easter Day or one of the three days thereafter. On the one hand, this placement seems to many people to make the observance of the Annunciation like the act of patting your head while rubbing your stomach. On the other hand, the announcement of the birth of the Savior by the grace of God is quite germane to the Lenten consideration of what it means to accept new life in Christ.

Although many Protestants are loathe to hear this, Mary is an important model for Christian discipleship. The number of times she is mentioned in the Gospels and the Acts far exceeds the number of references to most of the twelve disciples; it is difficult to contest that Luke, in particular, sees her as an important figure for the church, especially inasmuch as she is present at its establishment on the Day of Pentecost (Acts 1:14, 2:1).[14] In Orthodox Churches the great icon in the half-dome of the apse, directly above and behind the altar, depicts Jesus in the womb or on the lap of Mary. The inescapable message is: As Mary bore Christ physically into the world, so now the task of the church is to bear Christ spiritually into the world, so that all may believe. In that analogical sense, Mary is the premier model for what it means to be a Christian disciple. It is time for Protestants to put in perspective all the Reformation reaction against medieval distortions and to look afresh at the clues Mary may provide for what it means faithfully to fulfill the covenant with God. A hymn text from a recent time may be helpful in conveying the point:

> Blessed were the chosen people
> out of whom the Lord did come;
> blessed was the land of promise
> fashioned for his earthly home;
> but more blessed far the mother,
> she who bore him in her womb.
>
> Therefore let all faithful people
> sing the honor of her name;
> let the church, in her foreshadowed,
> part in her thanksgiving claim.[15]

The annunciation also raises the thorny question of the basic intent of the church's teaching about the virginal conception of Jesus (a more accurate term than "virgin birth"). At worst, this doctrine can be taken to imply that sexual intercourse is a nasty necessity for human procreation, but one from which the mother of Messiah can and must be extricated by miraculous action, lest her child be tainted. There is a far better possibility: that the unusual manner of Jesus' birth is to be seen as an enactment of meaning, as a sign of intense truth that cannot be revealed by ordinary activity. The Incarnation implies both divine and human agency. Far from being a way of avoiding connotations of lust, the virginal conception can be seen as a means of communicating the profoundness of divine love; it affirms how fully God's love is active among us. Just as the import of the resurrection of Jesus is ruined by a naive literalism, so also the significance of the birth of the savior. The work of God does not fit into our neat categories, but astonishes us by a creativity that uses means beyond our capacity to explain.

Visitation

Placed between the annunciation and the birth of John the Baptizer is the visit of Mary to the home of her relative Elizabeth, reported in Luke 1:39-56. The theme is exalted joy and fulfillment as the two women greet and express astonishment at the unexpected pregnancies that bring them together. Combined with the general theme of grace is an emphasis on the way in which God reverses human expectations and overturns commonly accepted values. For it is on this occasion that Mary sings her "Magnificat" (based on Hannah's song at the birth of Samuel), declaring that the mighty have been made low, and the lowly exalted; the hungry given a feast, and the rich sent away empty. (For unfathomable reasons, the Gospel assigned to this day in some lectionaries ends at Luke 1:47 or 49 rather than continuing to the end of the story at verse 56. There is no law against reading the whole account through to its conclusion.) The great exchange of divinity and humanity clearly results in exchanges of values within the human order.

Birth of John the Baptizer

The birth of Jesus, as we have seen, was placed in the calendar just after the shortest day of the year (in the northern hemisphere) to signal the One who is the world's true light. So the birth of John (reported in Luke 1:57-80) is located in proximity to the longest day of the year; this accords with the statement of the Baptizer concerning Jesus, "He must increase, but I must decrease" (John 3:30). Here also is an exchange of crucial importance. The function of the faithful Christian leader is to point to Christ and then stand aside—not to be the center of attention, let alone to be a mesmerizing figure to whom people are drawn as permanent disciples. (Recall the crucifixion scene from the Isenheim Altarpiece of Matthias Grünewald. The Baptizer, long dead before this event occurs, stands at the cross, forcefully pointing the index finger of his right hand at Jesus.) Thus John is a model of Christian leadership.

117

The Gospel reading for the occasion is rich both in its narrative detail and in the poetic affirmations of the Song of Zechariah, the father of John. Exactly half a year away from Christmas, this provides a good "refresher course" on the meaning of the coming of God into our midst.

The Name of Jesus

The fourth observance, and the only one that falls within the season of Christmas, concerns the Jewish rites occurring on the eighth day following birth as recorded in Luke 2:21. Though formerly known as "The Circumcision of Jesus," today this observance is more commonly called "The Name of Jesus"; accordingly, its focus has moved from an emphasis on the keeping of the ceremonial rites of Judaism to the meaning of the name "Jesus." Both interpretations, however, express the continuity of Judaism and Christianity; for "Jesus" is a form of "Joshua" and reveals Jesus as the one who leads us into the new land of milk and honey, as well as the one who saves (which the Hebrew form of "Joshua" or "Jeshua" connotes).

When observed on the actual date assigned to it (rather than on a nearby Sunday), this observance coincides with New Year's Day. The themes are compatible. Christ is the One who brings radical newness into our midst. And as January 1 and what follows cannot be severed from December 31 and what precedes, neither can Jesus be understood apart from the Jewish heritage of Mary and Joseph, who followed their traditions in the events celebrated on this day. Past and future are a continuum, with the present being the thin moving edge between them.

Presentation of Jesus

February 2, the fortieth day of the nativity, commemorates the presentation of Jesus in the temple (Luke 2:22-40) in accord with the legislation of Leviticus 12:2-8 concerning the firstborn male. Central to this occasion are the two great worthies, Simeon and Anna, whose patient faith is rewarded by great joy. The attribution of Simeon that Jesus shall be a light for revelation to the Gentiles inspired the custom of having a ceremony of candles at the Mass on this day; candles to be used throughout the next year were blessed on this occasion, and the faithful were given lighted candles, in token of the light of Christ. Hence the observance has been called "Candlemas."

That the day is commonly known as "Groundhog Day" is more than a source of amusement; it is something of a testimony to the enduring power of superstition even among those who say Christ is their light. News reporters, who have no clue to what the Presentation of Jesus is about, rush to see a furry rodent emerge from hibernation as a presumed omen concerning when winter will end. May this be an indicator of the great difficulty with which the Great Exchange comes into our lives? So much do folkways and superstition cling to us (witness the popularity of astrology) that we may find it impossible to believe we are "divinized" to any degree at all by virtue of the incarnation. Still, that must be the constant hope of Christians, undergirded by the ancient assurance that "we abide in him and he in us, because he has given us of his Spirit" (1 John 4:13).

6

Advent: The End and the Beginning

The First Sunday of Advent is regarded in the Western Church as the beginning of the liturgical year. But Advent is first of all about the end of time. Because the term itself means "coming" or "arrival," and because it precedes Christmas, many have misunderstood Advent to be exclusively a time to get ready to celebrate the coming of a child at Bethlehem. In fact, the primary focus of Advent is on what is popularly called "the second coming."[2] Thus Advent concerns the future of the Risen One, who will judge wickedness and prevail over every evil. Advent is the celebration of the promise that Christ will bring an end to all that is contrary to the ways of God; the resurrection of Jesus is the first sign of this destruction of the powers of death, the inauguration and anticipation of what is yet to come in fullness. As such, the opening Sundays of Advent bring to sharp focus themes that in the lectionary system have been accumulating for some weeks; for as the lectionary year closes, the Gospel readings, in particular, deal with signs of the end.

What may seem to be an anomaly is a very important theological point: The beginning of the liturgical year takes our thinking to the very end of things. For "end" means not only the "end of time," but the central purpose or goal of creation. We are not aimlessly wandering in a wilderness, even though we may be tempted to think so. Rather, history is headed somewhere by direction (though not dictation) from God. It is necessary that the liturgical year begin with this focus on a central, holy intention; for otherwise the story of Jesus, which is about to be rehearsed from conception and birth to death and resurrection, may seem less than what it is: the deliberate fulfilling of divine purpose, worked out through historical process. Only this focus on the central purpose of God in history can keep the story of Jesus from falling into the superstitious or almost magical understandings that often afflict the Christian community, on the one hand, or into the trivialization and irrelevance that characterize secular interpretations, on the other hand.

The intertwining of an ultimate goal and of the historical process that leads to that end establishes the otherwise puzzling design of the Advent season. We start the Advent observances with the future: "The reign of God is coming. Prepare!" We end with the past: "Messiah will be born in Bethlehem. Rejoice!" As we proceed across the four Sundays of the season both motifs are sounded; but the volume of the future emphasis declines as the sound level of the emphasis on the past increases. Apart from coming to terms with this design, it is impossible to make sense of the fact that the Gospel readings of Advent begin with a mature Jesus teaching about the reign of God, and close with an unborn Jesus, still in Mary's womb.

All of this is, however, a reverberation of what has been insisted on throughout this book: that the sacred story, to be understood aright, has to be read backward. Just as the birth and ministry of Jesus are incomprehensible until we know of the Lord's death and resurrection, so too the whole of the past is muddled unless first we have a grasp on the nature of the future. We turn now in a more detailed way to that seemingly backward Advent journey, week by week.

The First Sunday of Advent

On the opening Sunday, in each lectionary year we find Jesus proclaiming the end, but in a less than clearly defined way. The future holds surprises, for "no one knows the day or the hour." There will be signs that the end is at hand; even so, they can be missed by those who are not alert. Watchfulness is the key. In other words, God will faithfully fulfill the divine promise, but not necessarily in the way we suppose. This stands in judgment over the stance of many Christians who seem to have the end worked out in minute detail. Therefore beware of those who, as someone has quipped, presume "to know the furniture of heaven and the temperature of hell." For they do not in the least understand the ways of a God who keeps promises yet loves surprises.

Here there are subtle but crucial ties to the story of Bethlehem. The coming of Messiah occurred, but not in ways that most people would have expected. A few despised shepherds heard of it, while all of the proudly devout slept through it. When Gentiles from afar were clued in, the local religious scholars had to scurry to make sense of their questions. And ultimately Messiah was exalted by being placed high upon a cross—in part at least, as the result of having frustrated preconceived notions about what this agent of God ought to be doing in the world. These events from the past present us with a warning concerning the future: Watch lest you similarly miss the coming of the Lord!

At the same time, the lections for the First Sunday of Advent express a deep yearning for righteousness: "Come, let us walk / in the light of the LORD" (Isa. 2:5, Year A). "[O Lord,] you meet those who gladly do right, / those who remember you in your ways" (Isa. 64:5, Year B). "May the Lord make you increase and abound in love for one another and for all" (1 Thess. 3:12, Year C). Christian faith is less about precise knowledge of the future than about a passion for God's justice and holiness in the present, a passion that moves us both to action and to petition:

Send your Word, O Lord, like the rain, falling down upon the earth.
Send your Word.
We seek your endless grace,
with souls that hunger and thirst, sorrow and agonize.
We would all be lost in dark without your guiding light.

Send your Word, O Lord, like the wind, blowing down upon the earth.
Send your Word.
We seek your wondrous power,
pureness that rejects all sins, though they persist and cling.
Bring us to complete victory; set us all free indeed.

Send your Word, O Lord, like the dew, coming gently upon the hills.
Send your Word.
We seek your endless love.
For life that suffers in strife with adversities and hurts,
send your healing power of love; we long for your new world.[3]

The Second Sunday of Advent

A step backward in time: Last Sunday we saw Jesus well along in the ministry of teaching and healing. Today we hear the cry of the

Baptizer in the desert before the beginning of that teaching ministry. The Baptizer's cry can be strident. It is not enough to lay claim to a religious heritage ("We have Abraham as our ancestor"), nor even to profess repentance. The fruits of repentance are necessary; those who do not have them constitute a brood of vipers. But there is also promise in the Baptizer's message. Justice will be done. "There is one coming after me," says John, "who is more powerful than I am." The other readings for each Second Sunday are likewise filled with promise, strength, and hope. Righteousness shall reign on earth, with the lion and lamb dwelling together in peace; even the Gentiles will find their hope fulfilled (Year A). God will come with might, bringing new heavens and a new earth (Year B). The messenger of the Lord will purify all things, and a harvest of righteousness will be reaped (Year C).

It should be noted that these words of hope from various eras of Israel's life were typically penned in bleak times, even in the days of captivity in Babylon and in the decades of Roman occupation and early persecutions of the church. These words are not the glib musings of the comfortable but the trusting cries of those who see beyond the present dimness. The One in whom they have confidence has acted faithfully in the past and therefore is to be depended upon again and again. For the past reliability of God constitutes a promise for the future: God does not falter.

The Third Sunday of Advent

Another Sunday with the Baptizer, though in different settings from year to year. Whether we find him in prison or in the desert, always John is pointing forward to One who is to come. Christians are those who look forward and find God out ahead of them. The result is rejoicing, which characterizes this day, sometimes called "Gaudete Sunday." ("Gaudete" is a Latin imperative verb meaning "Rejoice!") Before Vatican II, Advent was interpreted more as a penitential season than it now is, a little Lent to be observed with much solemn prayer and fasting; but the Third Sunday was an easing off from this severity, and the rites began with the singing of Philippians 4:4-6 (now the epistle in Year C): "Rejoice in the Lord

124

always; again I will say, Rejoice. . . . The Lord is near." Even as the Baptizer demands strict repentance, we can be glad.

This is a necessary corrective to the common view that repentance is a chore and righteousness a means of removing all of the fun from life. Here is a recognition that the things usually trusted to bring human happiness are untrustworthy, even deceptive. Their pleasures are short-lived and frequently backfire on us. True joy lies elsewhere—in the work of God. This is an important caution at a time when Christmas happiness seems to depend upon gala parties, gaudy decorations, superficial holiday greeting cards, and musical ditties about a red-nosed reindeer. Even pious reminders that "Jesus is the reason for the season" may fail to confront us with the joy of repentance, of turning around and heading in a new direction of patient obedience to God, in whom alone there is true freedom and peace.

The Fourth Sunday of Advent

Only now do we step back far enough to hear something directly about the birth of the promised One. For the first time in Advent (and this may occur as late as December 24), we hear plainly that the confident but somewhat diffuse promises of earlier Sundays will find enfleshment in Mary's womb. This lingering of the Good News until the final Lord's Day of the season itself embodies the watchful patience that has been urged upon us for three weeks. The world around us simply cannot wait for Christmas to get here. Decorations for the season have been on sale in stores since September. By now most gifts have been purchased, some already presented, and a few undoubtedly used up or returned to the store for exchange. Santa Claus appeared in the flesh at least a month ago, possibly even coming from the heavens (via helicopter). But God plays a waiting game, keeping us on tiptoes. For even on this Fourth Sunday we are learning about how to wait patiently for the future reign of God, not only about how to wait for Christmas morning to arrive.

But the end leads to the beginning; at this point history has gained dominance over eschatology as the theme most clearly sounded in the Advent symphony. A child is to be born whose name is Emmanuel. Even while we await the day of the final reign of God, God is with us, in our midst. In some sense the God present with us waits for the end as impatiently as we wait. Not at all distant from the present struggle for justice, never removed from the present agony when justice is denied, this God is thoroughly engaged in both struggle and agony, yet always is ahead of us to ensure the victory. And so the church prays:

> Come, thou long-expected Jesus,
> born to set thy people free;
> from our fears and sins release us,
> let us find our rest in thee.
> Israel's strength and consolation,
> hope of all the earth thou art;
> dear desire of every nation,
> joy of every longing heart.[4]

This prayer directs us both toward the celebration of Christmas, now but a few days off, and toward the end of time, whose distance from us we cannot know; in all of that we pray for the present age, the thin moving edge that connects past to future. For always both the future and past emphases of Advent direct us toward our faith and mission in this world. Eschatology that has no implications for us now is pernicious escapism. History that has no implications for us now is irrelevant romanticism. Neither by escaping current responsibility, nor by retreating into a rosy past that never was, can we serve the God who has come and will come, yet is ever fully woven into the fabric of the present.

Ways of Marking Advent

Many worship practices done during Advent are more appropriately reserved for Christmas, and should be deferred where pastoral sensitivity can rearrange this effectively. Here are a few means of observance more directly in line with the themes of Advent itself.

Advent Wreath

A way of marking the progress of Advent that was little known fifty years ago is now almost universally accepted, even in churches that would insist they are "totally nonliturgical." This is the Advent

126

wreath, in which candles are lighted progressively, Sunday by Sunday. Because the wreath arose as a household custom in northern Europe, the church did not hedge it about with strict regulations (as likely would have been the case had its origin been the worship space of the congregation). Hence the forms of its use are so various as to be perplexing.

Sometimes instead of a wreath, an Advent "log" is used, in which candles are inserted in a straight line into a log rather than into a circular arrangement of greenery. This gets around the problem of whether to put up with phony greens or to have to replace fresh greens every two weeks or so; but at least to those of us who have participated in scouting, the log may be more reminiscent of an outdoor campfire ceremony of initiation than of Advent. Whatever form is used, in a place of worship the candles and their holder should be large enough to be visually significant. Too often wreaths designed to fit a dining-room table are brought into a space that seats two hundred or more people; the volume of the space in which they are set thereby overpowers the message the candles are intended to convey, causing the whole practice to seem trivial if not futile.

Some Advent wreaths have four candles, lighted progressively during Advent; thereafter the wreath is no longer used. Others have four colored candles on the four Advent Sundays; but on Christmas Eve four white candles are substituted and use continues throughout Christmas with all candles lighted. Still other wreaths have five candles, four in the outer ring and a fifth, larger candle (popularly called "the Christ candle") in the center. This fifth candle, of course, begins to be lighted only on Christmas Eve.

Nor is the color of the candles uniform. In the early stages of use, at least, often all four candles were white or perhaps red (for no better reason than that red and green connote Christmas). But an alternative was to use colors to match the liturgical color of the season. So four violet (or purple) candles came into use among Protestants. Shortly, however, even Protestant supply houses began to mimic an obsolete Roman Catholic custom; it had been the practice among Catholics to use rose (mistakenly called "pink") on Gaudete Sunday as a visual signal that the intense solemnity of the "violet Sundays" eased off for this occasion. So Advent kits are still sold containing three violet and one rose candle; never mind that Advent is no longer penitential in the Roman Church and that almost no one uses rose vestments! Most Protestants have no idea on which Sunday to light the "pink" candle for the first time, let alone why. Now that some denominations have gone to blue as the designated color for Advent, in those churches four blue candles may be used. Whatever practice is followed, it should be consistent from year to year.[5]

The primary reason for lighting one candle the First Sunday, that candle plus another on the Second Sunday, and so on, is to signal progression. The accumulation of light reminds us of the ever closer approach of the Light of the World, both at Bethlehem and in glory at the end of the age. Recently, however, another layer of symbolism has been added, without necessarily happy results. There has emerged the practice of giving a separate significance to each candle, so that the first represents, faith; the second, hope; the third, love; the fourth, joy. Or, faith, hope, love, and peace. Or humility, gentleness, patience, and kindness. Or various other sets of abstract virtues. Yet another system asserts that the first candle represents Mary and Joseph, the second the angels over Bethlehem's plain, the third the shepherds, and the fourth the Magi. Obviously this latter interpretation vitiates Advent by pulling Christmas back four Sundays. But all attempts to differentiate each candle with arbitrary designations obscure the basic symbol of accumulating light, and therefore probably are best abandoned.[6]

Chrismon Tree

This is another relatively recent addition to church symbolism and reflects a desire to give more significance to the use of Christmas trees in the worship area. "Chrismon" is a kind of contraction, combining the first five letters of "Christ" and the first three letters of the term "monogram." Actually only two sets of letters can be regarded as actual monograms. (1) The "Chi Rho," which looks to us like an "X" and a "P," is composed of the first two Greek letters of "Christ." (2) The "IHS" (composed not of English letters at all, but the Greek iota, eta, and sigma) is an abbreviation of the Greek name "Jesus." A third set of letters—the first and final of the Greek alphabet, Alpha and Omega—symbolizes the eternity of Christ (see Rev. 22:13). Beyond that the term "Chrismon" is used loosely to refer to symbols related to Christ, including the orb, crown, fish, star, anchor, and a wide variety of forms of the cross. All of these, often made in materials of gold and white, are used on a pine or fir tree in place of the more usual multicolored ornaments used on trees at home. Lights also are usually of clear glass rather than being colored.

A variation involves the use of two contrasting trees, one on either side of the center of the worship area. The other tree is a dead deciduous tree, either barren or with withered brown leaves. This tree thus represents the old life of death through sin, while the Chrismon tree represents our new life in Christ. The symbolism is mitigated, however, when the Chrismon tree is an artificial tree, as is often the case since the tree is to be displayed over a long period; the symbolism is strained if one tree that was alive is now dead, while the other pretends to be alive but never can be.

Because many symbols of the Chrismon tree direct our attention to the nature and ultimate work of Christ, rather than primarily to Bethlehem, they can be helpful in calling attention to Advent themes. Often their symbolism is esoteric and may be lost on many in the congregation unless accompanied by clear interpretation. Careful teaching week by week (perhaps printed in the service folder or church newsletter) may bring appropriate Advent themes to the fore.

"O" Antiphons

At least equally esoteric, but also worth the labor of careful interpretation, are seven brief prayers, each of which begins with a vocative "O." In churches that hold daily services of Evening Prayer, these are sung sequentially from December 17 to 23 as the response to the *Magnificat* in that rite; hence the name "antiphon," meaning sung response.

The "Great O's," as they are sometimes called, can readily be used in other ways. For example, two can be used on each Sunday of Advent, perhaps one near the beginning of the service and one near its close; or preceding and following the First Reading; or at the lighting of the Advent candles. The "O Emmanuel" antiphon can be used twice (on the First and Fourth Sundays) to create the full complement of eight. Or, all seven can be read in sequence each Sunday.

The antiphons are rich with biblical allusions that are sometimes unfamiliar to us, but that can be used in Advent teaching and preaching. Below are the antiphons; a leader may recite the portions printed in roman type with the congregation making the petition printed in italics. The citations of texts that gave rise to the antiphons are to the right, together with lectionary correspondences, where these apply.[7]

1. O WISDOM,

coming forth from the mouth of the Most High,	Sirach (Ecclesiasticus) 24:3
reaching from one end of the earth to the other:	
You order all things well with strength and gentleness.	Wisdom of Solomon 8:1
Come and teach us the way of knowledge.	

2. O ADONAI,

leader of the house of Israel:	Psalm 46:3; Acts 2:36
You appeared to Moses in the burning bush,	Exodus 3:2ff.
and at Sinai gave him the Law.	Exodus 20:1-17
Come and redeem us by your outstretched arm.	Exodus 6:6

3. O ROOT OF JESSE:

You stand as a signal before your people.	Isaiah 11:10 [2A]
Monarchs close their mouths because of you;	Isaiah 52:15
to you all nations shall bow.	Psalm 102:15
Come and deliver us without delay.	Habakkuk 2:3

4. O KEY OF DAVID and scepter of Israel:

You open and no one shall shut;	Isaiah 22:22;
you shut and no one shall open.	Psalm 110:2;
	Revelation 3:7
Come and release from the prison house those	Isaiah 42:7;
who sit in darkness, in the shadow of death.	Luke 1:79 [2C]

5. O DAWN from on high,

	Luke 1:78 [2C]
splendor of God's light and sun of justice:	Malachi 4:2
Come and enlighten those who sit in darkness,	
in the shadow of death.	Luke 1:79 [2C]

6. O RULER of the Gentiles,

their treasure	Haggai 2:7
and the cornerstone that binds them in	Isaiah 28:16;
one:	Ephesians 2:14, 20

Come and save those whom you formed   Genesis 2:7
   from the dust.

7. O IMMANUEL,   Isaiah 7:14; 8:8 [4A]
our ruler and lawgiver,   Isaiah 33:22
the expectation and savior of the nations: Luke 3:15 [3C]
Come and set us free, O Lord our God.

Seasonal Music

There are many alternatives to the common free church practice
of beginning to sing Christmas carols on the First Sunday of Advent.
Recently issued hymnals have many more Advent selections than
their predecessors; often hymnals have "hidden" hymns, those that
are categorized not under "Advent" but under a heading such as
"the reign of God" or "the return of the Lord."[8]

The texts of the "O Antiphons" are the basis of the well-known
Advent hymn "O Come, O Come, Emmanuel." While older hymnals
have often abridged that text, several recent hymnals (including Episcopal and United Methodist) provide all seven stanzas. Two stanzas
can be sung each week, as suggested above for the spoken texts.

Solos and anthems from Handel's *Messiah* are much used during
Advent. All selections in that oratorio preceding "the Pastoral Symphony" (that is, nos. 2-12) proclaim Hebrew texts, many of which are
found in the lectionary selections for Advent. But later portions are also
quite appropriate for Advent, including 19-23, 32, 38-42, and 50. Since
the whole first division of *Messiah* is popularly thought of as "Christmas
music," using the selections designated here is one way of eating your
cake and having it, too. Those who plan the service know these texts
are about Advent, not Christmas; but many who hear them will be
satisfied that this is "Christmas" music and will not go home muttering,
"Why is it our worship planners don't know it is Christmas?"

From King's College, Cambridge, England, comes not only a
service of lessons and carols for Christmas but a corollary service for
Advent I. This also can be adapted effectively for use at any point
throughout Advent.[9]

However it is achieved, worship during Advent should ever
clearly and forcefully proclaim the fullness of the coming of Christ
into our midst—future, past, and present.

7

Ordinary and Extraordinary Time

More than one-half of the liturgical year is categorized under the heading "Ordinary Time." The intention behind this wording is easily misunderstood by all except the few who remember what their math teachers told them about two different ways of counting: by cardinal numbers (one, two, three, four) and by ordinal numbers (first, second, third, fourth). "Ordinary Time" implies no mundaneness, as if more than half the year were dull and unexciting; it refers to the fact that in the original lectionary system the Sundays outside Advent-Christmas and Lent-Easter were simply designated by ordinal numbers: First Sunday, Second Sunday, and on through to the Thirty-fourth Sunday.[1] In the weeks between Epiphany and Lent, as many of these sets of lessons were used as the calendar for that year required; then after Pentecost (or Trinity Sunday, which follows it), the ordinal Sundays were taken up where they had been left off at the start of Lent. And so things continued until Advent.

Contrasts and Complementarity

Because of the use of ordinals to designate its Sundays, the title "Ordinary Time" is technically accurate, if a bit misleading or confusing. Often, however, truth is revealed unwittingly, in what we popularly refer to as "Freudian slips." The reason "ordinary" is taken to mean "unexciting" is that this is precisely how many have come to regard more than half the liturgical year: During certain times we commemorate the great moments in the coming of Christ; and the rest of the time is, well, rather ordinary. We just go on about our business with nothing so edifying as Christmas or Easter or Pentecost to celebrate.

Nor is this interpretation wholly bad. The excitement of life often depends on the principle of contrast by alternation. If every evening at dinner time you are served a great banquet of fine foods in lavish surroundings, soon none of those events seems particularly exciting. Banquets have significance by their contrast with what happens on most other evenings. So, too, in church. Advent builds up gradually toward the peak of Christmas Day and the high plateau that forms the rest of the Christmas season. Following is a pause, a relaxation, until Lent. Then there is again the intensifying anticipation of Lent, fulfillment in Easter Day and its great season, and relaxation until Advent. If Easter Day or Christmas Day occurred every week, would we not tire of them quickly?

All of that is quite true psychologically. But theologically something else entirely is occurring. Because of what has been made known in Christ, no time can again be regarded as ordinary in the sense of dull or commonplace. The liturgical calendar as a whole exists in large part to remind us that Christ has sanctified all of time, bringing us and the whole of our experience into the orbit of resurrection. What we deem ordinary, God has transformed into the extraordinary by the power of divine grace.

This does not mean that all of our experiences or perceptions of the world are positive and happy, or that we are set free from all weakness, struggle, and evil. On the contrary, the extraordinariness of God's work is seen amid our anxiety, fear, and perplexity. God works in the midst of adversity and in spite of it, not in its absence. That is why the resurrection can never be separated from the cross which precedes it.

Even from this theological perspective, contrast by alternation is at work. For nearly half the year we come to know the work of God through the great events of our sacred history. During the rest of the year we come to know the work of God in the world that is closer to us in time and space. Claus Westermann has helpfully distinguished between two complementary aspects of divine work: (1) salvation, or God's saving, rescuing activity seen in great epiphanies; and (2) blessing, or God's less dramatic but equally important continuing presence. These two are not contradictory or even completely distinct. Both are needed for a full apprehension of divine grace.[2]

Nor can we even distinguish these elements sharply from Sunday to Sunday or season to season. Always they interpenetrate each other. It would be outrageous to suppose that the drama of divine rescue is not to be proclaimed during Ordinary Time or that the quieter evidences of God's presence should be overlooked during the great fanfare of Easter celebrations. But God's saving acts are more likely to come to the fore during the occasions marked by the great Easter and Christmas cycles, while God's less obvious continuing presence may grasp our attention more readily at other times.

Attention to the need for contrast by alternation may well be signaled to the congregation in ways that alert worshipers to such differences. A simple suggestion: During the two great cycles, designate the Sundays according to their context in those cycles: December 22, Third Sunday of Advent; March 30, Fifth Sunday in Lent; and so on. But in Ordinary Time use no designation more complicated than "Sunday, October 10." Sunday stands on its own as the Lord's Day; it does not need a secondary designation to give it meaning. By this simple practice, we may be reminded that God's grace is recognized in differing ways at varying times, to our great benefit.

A week-by-week commentary on Ordinary Time is not possible here; that is the task of a book on the lectionary as such. The themes throughout Ordinary Time vary from week to week within each cycle as well as across the cycles of Years A, B, and C. Suffice it to say that in Ordinary Time we should be particularly aware of, and thankful for, the work of God in our midst on every sort of occasion. The God who is made known in the obvious events surrounding the life, death, and resurrection of Jesus is no less made known in transforming power in every experience common to humanity. However, because of human frailty we may not be inclined to recognize God's action in our midst day by day. We will therefore need to ask that our eyes be opened more fully to all of the evidences of God's grace that are presented to us.

Transitional Sundays

Certain occasions in Ordinary Time can be interpreted as transitions into and out of the two great cycles, though not all denominations would so understand them, or even observe all of them.

Transfiguration Sunday

The observance of the Transfiguration on the Sunday prior to Ash Wednesday is not universal. Roman Catholics retain this day in its old location on August 6, but also read the Transfiguration narrative on the Second Sunday of Lent. But moving the commemoration from an August weekday to the Sunday before Lent (as many Protestants now do) has much to commend it. For the transfiguration can thereby act as a bridge into Lent by further identifying who Jesus is and by anticipating what will occur in Jerusalem.[3]

First, in the transfiguration narratives, Jesus' conversation with Moses and Elijah is theological personification. Moses represents Torah (the Law), Elijah the Prophets. The latter identification is often veiled from Christians, who must be reminded that in the Hebrew canon the category of "the Prophets" begins not with Isaiah (as in the Christian canon) but with Joshua, Judges, 1 and 2 Samuel, and 1 and 2 Kings. Elijah is thereby properly regarded as a premier representative of the prophets. Thus when talking to Moses and Elijah on the mountain, Jesus is in dialogue and continuity with the whole of the scriptures as they were then codified. (The third division of the Hebrew canon, the Writings, was not firmly established until well after the time the Synoptics were written.)

Luke specifies what the three on the mountain were discussing: Jesus' "departure," about to be accomplished at Jerusalem (9:31). English translations typically blunt the force of the Greek term, which is "exodus." "Exodus" literally means "the road out," in this case implying Jesus' death; but the choice of wording must have been a deliberate tactic by Luke to tie together the signal saving acts of God for Jews and Christians: As God through Moses led Israel out of bondage to Pharaoh by the Exodus, so God in Christ leads us from sin's bondage by way of the cross.

If the conversation on the mountain points to the crucifixion, the glistening appearance of Jesus prefigures the resurrection. Dazzling brightness is another form of theological shorthand; it commonly has eschatological reference. (The Revelation again and again refers to the brightness of garments in heaven.) There are further eschatological connections between Moses, Elijah, and Jesus. The face of Moses shone after he talked with God at Sinai, and Elijah was taken into heaven in a kind of ascension. The readings from the Hebrew Scriptures appointed in the lectionary for Transfiguration Sunday make use of these associations.

Who is this who was born in Bethlehem and now is steadfastly headed for Jerusalem? This is the One who by being crucified and raised will fulfill all that the scriptures have promised. Before the curtain goes up on the action of a dramatic opera, the orchestra plays an overture that hints at the musical themes to follow; so, just before the opening of Lent, the transfiguration presents subtle clues to the content of the Forty Days of Devotion and Discipline and the Great Fifty Days of rejoicing that follow.

Trinity Sunday

As transfiguration eases us into the Lent-Easter complex, the Sunday of the Trinity can be seen as a transition between this complex and Ordinary Time. The observance, however, presents difficulties and challenges.

Placement at the end of the cycle of the commemorations of events from Advent to Pentecost has wrongly led some to consider Trinity Sunday a day on which to celebrate the "completion" of the revelation of the Trinity. This misinterpretation has two manifestations: (1) Displacement, in which it is supposed the First Person of the Trinity existed from creation until Bethlehem, the Second from Bethlehem until the Ascension, and the Third Person from the Day of Pentecost forward. This recapitulates the ancient heresy of modalism (also called monarchianism, or Sabellianism), in which God is shown in turn in three different guises or modes. (2) Accumulation, in which the revelation of the Second Person is added to that of the First Person at the point of the incarnation, and the Third Person is added to the other two at Pentecost.

Orthodox trinitarian interpretations insist that all three Persons exist together from all eternity to all eternity. The Trinity cannot know incompleteness. Trinitarianism is in fact a way of affirming that God *is* completeness, and that all existence proceeds from the fullness of God. This is likely one of the reasons that Trinity Sunday had no general observance in the Western Church until 1334. Indeed in the eleventh century, Pope Alexander II resisted the observance of Trinity Sunday, saying that the Trinity in its fullness is honored on every day of the church year, and that a discrete observance could serve only to obscure this fact.

At the other end of the spectrum, it can readily be supposed that far from having to do with events at all, Trinity Sunday arises from a doctrine not an occasion. Doctrines are exceedingly important in Christian faith, but from the perspective we are now addressing they are to be understood as systematic reflections that grow out of events; and thereby they may be difficult to turn into liturgical celebrations. (Or, to give it a cute twist: Liturgical observances rooted in doctrines rather than events are more likely to be "cerebrations" than "celebrations.")

That viewpoint contains both an insight and an error. Certainly it is true that the doctrine of the Trinity does not grow out of one discrete occasion in the way in which Christmas Day springs from the event of the nativity. But neither does Trinity Sunday arise apart from the whole complex of occasions celebrated in the liturgical year. It is clear in Luke's theology, for example, that by the will of God the Holy Spirit is active in the conception of Jesus. The narratives of Jesus' baptism may not fully outline a trinitarian system such as that articulated by the councils of the first four centuries; but to deny trinitarian assumptions in those stories is to handle the texts violently. The same case can be made with respect to any number of incidents in the story of Jesus. Trinitarianism, while clearly a doctrinal assertion, nevertheless is grounded in the narratives of faith that are celebrated throughout the liturgical calendar.

So what should be done with Trinity Sunday? Certainly it is not wise to try to have an annual observance that by its grandeur detracts from the Great Fifty Days. Still, trinitarian theology is so crucial and so misunderstood by most people in the pews (and many in the pulpit) that the occurrence of this date in the calendar may be a way of reminding us to take seriously this teaching and to present it in ways that communicate both solid content and joyous thanksgiving. Rather than seeming to signal the end (and completion) of a sequence of events, Trinity Sunday may be a time to reflect on how the fullness of God has been at work throughout the entire story that the year commemorates. Thus Trinity Sunday becomes an occasion for recapitulation and acts as an appropriate transition into Ordinary Time.

Christ the King Sunday

This occasion acts as a bridge from the last Sundays of Ordinary Time, with their Gospel readings about the signs of the end, to the futuristic tone of Advent.[4] An alternative title for the day is "Reign of Christ Sunday"; this bypasses objections to references to monarchy that seem to include only male rulers or that seem to give too much weight to the maleness of Jesus. Sometimes, however, objections to the title "Christ the King" operate at a level that involves governmental rather than gender analogies: Is it appropriate for Christians committed to democratic forms of government to refer to God as a reigning monarch? Should not the monarchical metaphor be replaced in such instances by a democratic one? Although such questions initially have appeal, it is necessary to note the serious limitations of imagery for God drawn from democratic forms of government.

Democracies take for granted the undependability of those who govern within them. That is why checks and balances are built into such systems; it is simply assumed that if one person gets too much power for too long, injustice is bound to arise. Such a person inevitably develops into a tyrant and corruption becomes an unalterable way of life. Furthermore, the electorate is fickle and prone to bad judgment. Given these assumptions and characteristics of democracy, do we really wish to pursue the analogy of God as president or prime minister of the universe? Such language makes God subject to the whims of the electorate every four years (under the form of government in the United States), or anytime a vote of confidence fails (under the British parliamentary system).

Furthermore, several things about the character of God that cannot be relinquished are missing from democratic assumptions. When taken into account, these assertions ameliorate the main problems we have in thinking of Christ as a reigning monarch. (1) God, unlike earthly rulers, is just and can be trusted completely. There is with God no abuse of power, no compromising with injustice, no secret "deals" or oppressive tactics. (2) This righteousness of God cannot be altered by the whims of anyone. God is sovereign; if we stand opposed to the justice of God, it is we who will either bend to the divine will or be judged and set aside by its holiness. (3) Therefore all the frustrations and imperfections of the human struggle to achieve goodness are obliterated in God's activity. Divine justice ultimately has its way, no matter how long that may seem to take or how great our difficulty in believing that it will occur.

In the end, no metaphor drawn from human systems of government is adequate for God. But since we have no other metaphors from which to draw other than those of our own experience, the use of royal language for God is still the most useful we have found.

That leads to a further characteristic of theology as metaphorical language: Despite the fact that metaphors begin with our experience and are used by us to attempt to articulate the nature of God (which we can never fully articulate), by grace the process ultimately is reversed. God's reign becomes a kind of metaphor by which to judge and on which to base human behavior. Talk about the reign of God makes apparent the deficiencies of human rulers and provides clues as to what might make human governance more just. As a transition into Advent, the Sunday devoted to the reign of Christ enables us to grasp more fully the Advent promise of the One who shall be called "the Prince of peace" and presses upon us the need to "seek peace and pursue it" (1 Pet. 3:11).

Baptism of the Lord

The content of this occasion has been discussed in chapter 5. Whether it is to be construed as a transitional Sunday from Christmas into Ordinary Time, or whether it should be regarded as a more intimate part of Christmas can be debated. To those who like things neat and tidy, having a transitional Sunday at each end of the Advent-Christmas cycle may have great appeal. But the point is hardly worth extensive argumentation.

All of the transitional occasions can be helpful in guiding us from place to place within the calendar system. None has the status of the high festival days, yet each in some ways augments the meaning of those days and presents us with yet another facet of the resurrection power of the One whose name we bear as Christian people. In that capacity as the people of God, we are called and enabled to discover God at work, day in and day out, such that time, otherwise apt to be regarded as ordinary, assumes for us extraordinary significance.

140

8

The Sanctoral Cycle: Resurrection Power in Human Lives

"Sanctoral" pertains to sanctity and sanctification. The Sanctoral Cycle celebrates the lives of the saints. Almost at once it will be objected that "Protestants do not have saints." Yet by opening my local phone directory I can readily find listings for St. Francis Episcopal Church, St. James Baptist Church, St. John's Lutheran Church, St. Paul's Moravian Church, John Knox Presbyterian Church, John Wesley African Methodist Episcopal Church, Francis Asbury United Methodist Church, and Luther Rice Memorial Baptist Church. Congregations name their social halls and societies after Martin Luther, John Calvin, Susanna Wesley, Barbara Heck, Richard Allen, Frances Willard, Sojourner Truth, Jane Addams, Martin Luther King, Jr., and Dorothy Day. Of course Protestants have saints, just as do the Orthodox and Roman Catholics. The writer of this hymn has it exactly right: "Rejoice in God's saints, today and all days; / a world without saints forgets how to praise."[1]

That poetic specification of "God's saints" is perceptive on two counts. First, there are plenty of secular saints in vogue, though we may refer to them as "role models," as "cultural heroes and heroines," or even (with more candor than we know) as "idols."[2] These include stars from the world of sports and entertainment, political leaders, moguls of business and industry, and sometimes criminals. As human beings we need persons whom we can revere; for Christians these should be chosen from the examples of godly living that abound in our history. But too often these examples are barely known, if at all. The sanctoral calendar is an effective way of keeping worthy mentors before Christian people.

Second, and of greater importance, is the poet's insight that those we rightly revere are "God's saints" in the sense that God creates them by grace. Men and women do not by sheer determination and self-discipline become saints. Sanctity is a divine gift. It is indeed the power of the resurrection at work in human lives. Thus commemorating the saints is nothing other than a way of affirming that the transformative power of Christ is at work all about us in human lives. By looking at particular instances that are, we might say, "high profile" persons, we are the better able to identify that transforming work in those we meet every day—and in ourselves.

For the term "saint" is not limited to the "greats" of history. The New Testament uses the term synonymously with "Christian" or "believer." Paul's use of the word is at points astounding if not shocking. Recall all of the difficulties he had with the church at Corinth and the many aberrations of faithful discipleship found among its members. Nevertheless, Paul addresses all the members of the Corinthian church as saints. This is in itself an indication that sanctity is attributed to Christ.

Therein we find hope for ourselves. We are saints because God's sanctity is at work in us, not because on our own we have come to great spiritual attainment. In exploring the lives of the historic saints, it is necessary to be thoroughly honest about their limitations and faults, for only in this way do we come to believe that God can also work in the people around us and even in us, whose faults we know fully well. It is no service to God to depict the great Christians of the ages as if they had no weaknesses, suffered no doubts, were afflicted with no prejudices, committed no sins, and never engaged in a serious struggle against forces about to overwhelm them. On the contrary.

Recall the report of the Apostle to those same Corinthians, concerning how he had wrestled in vain with what he calls "a thorn in the flesh." He asked God to remove it, but back came this reply, "My grace is sufficient for you, for power is made perfect in weakness." Therefore, concluded Paul, "I will boast all the more gladly of my weaknesses, so that the power of Christ may dwell in me. Therefore I am content with weaknesses, insults, hardships, persecutions, and calamities for the sake of Christ; for whenever I am weak, then I am strong" (2 Cor. 12:9-10). Therein is the New Testament definition of sanctity that defines the nature of the sanctoral cycle.

142

Design and Use of the Cycle

In relation to the calendar as we have discussed it thus far, the sanctoral cycle is an overlay. The day of a saint's commemoration is not determined by the season within which it is located (except as noted below with relation to the days of Stephen, John, and the Holy Innocents). Sometimes a saint's day will coincide with, and thus be displaced by, some event of greater significance. For example, St. Anselm, the medieval theologian who was Archbishop of Canterbury, is given April 21. In 2011 that date will be Holy Thursday and in 2019 will be Easter Day. In instances of such collisions, Anselm's observance will be transferred to another occasion or else will not be observed in those years. Nor (except among some Lutherans) does a saint's day take precedence over the Lord's Day, for reasons that should be obvious. Denominations that have formal sanctoral calendars also have clearly established rules of precedence that can be consulted for direction and that need not be considered in detail here.

Whenever possible, a holy person is given the date in the sanctoral cycle that corresponds to the day of that person's death, not the day of physical birth. The death day has traditionally been known as "the day of birth into eternity" and is thus given the greater significance. But care is taken not to have a day shared by unrelated saints. Thus when John Wesley was added to the commemorations of Anglicans, he could not be given his death day, March 2, since that had long ago been designated to honor Chad, Bishop of Lichfield in the seventh century; therefore John (together with his brother Charles) were assigned March 3, the next available date. But in the calendar of United Methodists (who have no particular devotion to Chad), John Wesley is assigned March 2, and Charles is rightly given a separate commemoration on his death day, March 29.

Sanctoral calendars do properly vary widely from denomination to denomination and even from country to country within the same denomination. There is, however, an agreed upon core, based on biblical saints. Following the secular calendar year (which is how the sanctoral cycle is generally set forth), the days of the New Testament commemorations are:

January 18	The Confession of Peter
January 25	The Conversion of Paul
February 24	Matthias, Apostle
March 19	Joseph, husband of Mary
April 25	Mark, Evangelist
May 1	Philip and James the Less, Apostles
June 11	Barnabas, Apostle
June 29	Peter and Paul, Apostles
July 22	Mary Magdalene
July 25	James the Elder, Apostle
August 15	Mary, the Mother of Jesus
August 24	Bartholomew, Apostle
September 21	Matthew, Evangelist and Apostle
October 18	Luke, Evangelist
October 23	James of Jerusalem, Brother of Jesus, Martyr
October 28	Simon and Jude, Apostles
November 30	Andrew, Apostle
December 21	Thomas, Apostle
December 26	Stephen, Deacon and Martyr
December 27	John, Evangelist and Apostle
December 28	Holy Innocents of Bethlehem, Martyrs

Several comments on this basic calendar are noteworthy: (1) Since the death dates of persons in the New Testament period are not known, convenience has tended to dictate placement. Hence there are few of these days that collide with Easter and related events. (2) Peter and Paul share a day, thereby indicating the dependence of the church on these two stalwarts who did not exactly see eye to eye while alive! But because of their preeminence, each is separately commemorated in January for a particular event: the confession of Peter at Caesarea Philippi, "You are Messiah [the Christ]"; and the conversion of Paul on the road to Damascus. In recent times the eight days embracing these two observances have become "the Octave of Christian Unity," a time to reckon with the division of the Church and the need to restore its wholeness, despite differences of opinions such as those that characterized the two apostles themselves.

Again, because death dates were not known, three biblical commemorations were given special status by their unusual placement in the sanctoral cycle. The question seems to have been raised: "Who by way of honor should be assigned their birth days into eternity by being placed immediately after the celebration of the earthly birth day of their Savior?" The answer that evolved provides a concise glimpse into the nature of the calendar itself.[3]

The date of greatest honor in relation to the birth of Jesus is, of course, the next day, December 26. And who could be considered greater than the first believer recorded to have laid down his life for the faith: Stephen the deacon, whose martyrdom is recounted in Acts 6:5–8:2. Willingness to die for the faith was so ultimate a proof of faithfulness in the ancient church that catechumens who suffered martyrdom were regarded as having been baptized in their own blood, even though they had not yet been granted baptism in water.

Still, it was a bit odd that the day after Christmas should not have been given to one of the apostles, all of whom except John are believed to have been martyred. So should not an apostle be given December 27? Certainly, but which? Ought it not to be the one the Fourth Gospel says was particularly loved by Jesus—even though he was the very one who escaped martyrdom (though presumably as a reward for having been the only one who did not desert Jesus as the crucifixion approached)? And so it is.

And what about December 28? There great theological inventiveness took over. Granted Stephen was the first person explicitly martyred for the faith. But had not a host given their lives long before in order that the faith might come into being? Thus the young males who were slaughtered by order of King Herod after the Magi had come inquiring about the birth of Messiah were given a special honor: They were regarded as unintended martyrs and granted December 28 as the "Feast of the Holy Innocents."

Quaint as the whole design seems at first glance, upon further reflection it has profound meaning. There are the great and evident saints: Some will actually die rather than renounce the faith. Others will not be called upon to be martyrs but will give stunning evidence of their faithfulness by their consistent devotion and obedience. Still others will serve Christ in ways barely recognized and will not themselves know that they are doing so. Very few of us will ever have opportunity to fall into the first category, and many of us will not even qualify for the second. Still, perhaps in ways we do not comprehend, in lives readily forgotten or deemed by others absurdly insignificant, we too serve the purposes of God. God calls all kinds in order to constitute the goodly company of the saints.

The older forms of the sanctoral cycle were dominated by males, and often by males of one particular ethnic, national, or denominational tradition. Recent revisions of the calendar have gone a long way toward changing that narrowness, and continuing efforts are to be commended with fervor.

Calendars are constituted in varying ways. Roman Catholics require a very elaborate process of investigation and official canonization before a person can be called "saint." Both the Orthodox and Protestants are less formal about the matter. Popularity and general consensus determine their approaches. Within Protestantism itself different practices prevail. Anglicans have always held to the commemoration of biblical saints; the last half of the twentieth century has seen great expansion (and much diversity) by the various branches of that communion. Many Lutherans, too, now have very ample sanctoral calendars. On the other hand, neither the 1992 *United Methodist Book of Worship* nor the 1993 *Book of Common Worship* of the joint Presbyterian bodies contains a sanctoral system.[4]

How fully should the sanctoral cycle be observed? It all depends. Certainly never should any part of it obscure the centrality of the Lord's Day or compete with the cycles of Lent-Easter or Advent-Christmas. Observances on weekdays are increasingly difficult to carry off in our hectic society. But at least a start can be made, including Sunday references that do not obscure the focus of that day. It is ironic and tragic that congregations who have named themselves after a biblical saint or later church leader may have no idea when that person is commemorated in the calendar, and probably know equally little about why their congregation bears that name. (Often congregations named "St. John's" cannot even tell you whether it is the Baptizer, the son of Zebedee, or the author of the Gospel who is being commemorated.)

Allow a modest suggestion at a point of convergence between what is commonly called "the children's sermon" in the Sunday service and the need to present young people with worthy models for Christian living. Rather than relying on cute tricks, or analogies (which children are incapable of grasping), use the children's time as an opportunity to teach Christian biography. Given the diversity of recent sanctoral systems, week by week both children and adults (who have largely been denied this in their own upbringing) can be told of faithful women and men from many eras, cultures, denominations, and situations in life. The effect upon Christian living could be surprisingly salutary.

While irrational reactions to Roman Catholicism can deter the use of the sanctoral cycle, prejudicial assumptions should not be made. Some years ago I was invited to preach at "St. Mary's United Methodist Church" in the southernmost part of West Virginia. I blithely assumed that of course this congregation could not be named for the mother of Jesus but must be situated on a St. Mary's River or in St. Mary's County. The truth astounded and delighted me. At the time of the reunion of the three Methodist denominations in 1939, this town found itself with two congregations that after merger into The Methodist Church would have had the same name. They drew straws, and the congregation that was to become St. Mary's had the task of finding a new designation for itself. In the ensuing discussion, the men of the church confessed, "During the depression we were ready to close this place down and join one of the other Methodist congregations in town. It was the women who insisted otherwise; and they kept us alive by bake sales, quilting bees, bazaars, and church suppers. Perhaps we should name our church after a woman." More discussion followed, in the course of which the pastor (quite a radical, apparently) said, "Well, how about the foremost woman in the New Testament, the mother of Jesus?" And so in 1939, a congregation in rural West Virginia, despite much prevailing anti-Catholic sentiment, willingly renamed itself "Saint Mary's Methodist Church." Honest to God!

The Festival of All Saints

One occasion in the sanctoral cycle cries out for special consideration. Given the widespread persecution in the early centuries, it did not take long for every date in the secular calendar to be assigned to one, and then to several, martyrs. Eventually a crisis developed, and a solution arose: Designate one day each year as a kind of omnibus occasion, a day on which to commemorate all the saints who cannot be accorded their own specific dates, and whose names have often been forgotten. In the West this "All Saints Day" settled down to November 1. (Orthodoxy better preserves the link between the Lord's resurrection and our sanctification by putting the observance on May 13 in some rites and on the Sunday following the Day of Pentecost in others.)

Because of its strictures noted above, in the Roman Catholic Church only officially canonized saints are commemorated on November 1, and all other faithful departed are remembered with almost equal solemnity on November 2. Protestants have collapsed the two occasions into one. This being the case, All Saints Day is less about the great historic figures of the church than about people we ourselves have known and revered. It is not uncommon for an All Saints Day observance (usually moved to the first Sunday in November) to include the reading of the names of all in the congregation who have died in the past year; memorial gifts in their honor may also be dedicated on this occasion. As an added consideration, because this day is likely to be more distant from death than the funeral, survivors have begun to work through their grief and can hear the resurrection hope with greater clarity.

Such commemorations should not be limited by time or parish boundaries, however. The All Saints observance is a time when all can reflect on and give thanks for deceased persons who have been influential in their spiritual formation and growth. As a result, all are reminded of the influence their lives can have upon others. This in turn may strengthen our resolve to lead lives worthy of imitation, to open ourselves more fully to the sanctifying power of God. An All Saints hymn originally written only for the edification of the poet's children makes the point:

> I sing a song of the saints of God,
> patient and brave and true,
> who toiled and fought and lived and died
> for the Lord they loved and knew.
> And one was a doctor, and one was a queen,
> and one was a shepherdess on the green;
> they were all of them saints of God, and I mean,
> God helping, to be one too.
>
> They lived not only in ages past;
> there are hundreds of thousands still.

148

> The world is bright with the joyous saints
> who love to do Jesus' will.
> You can meet them in school, on the street, in the store,
> in church, by the sea, in the house next door;
> they are saints of God, whether rich or poor,
> and I mean to be one too.[5]

All Saints Day also emphasizes the unity of the church across time. It reminds us that, as G. K. Chesterton is said to have observed, "If you want to know the size of the church, you have to count tombstones." In doing that, we are also notified of our own death and hope of life:

> Come, let us join our friends above
> who have obtained the prize,
> and on the eagle wings of love
> to joys celestial rise.
> Let saints on earth unite to sing
> with those to glory gone,
> for all the servants of our King
> in earth and heaven are one.
>
> One family we dwell in him,
> one church above, beneath,
> though now divided by the stream,
> the narrow stream of death;
> one army of the living God,
> to his command we bow;
> part of his host have crossed the flood,
> and part are crossing now.
>
> Ten thousand to their endless home
> this solemn moment fly,
> and we are to the margin come,
> and we expect to die.
>
> . . . .
>
> O that we now might grasp our Guide!
> O that the word were given!
> Come, Lord of Hosts, the waves divide,
> and land us all in heaven.[6]

149

Somewhat off to itself about a month before Advent, All Saints Day in a rather impressive way pulls together themes from the entire liturgical calendar: the work of resurrection grace in all of God's people; the devotion and discipline needed in the life obedient to God; the divinization of our humanity by the incarnation of divinity, accomplished by the power of the Spirit; the connectedness of all believers; the hope of life beyond death. It is all implicitly there; for the heart of the gospel, after all, is about God grasping us in such a way as to transform sinners into saints.

Karen Blixen-Finecke once observed, "All sorrows can be borne if you put them into a story or tell a story about them."[7] Life is full of sorrow as well as joy, of tribulation as surely as triumph. If all sorrows can indeed be borne by means of stories, how much more true this must be for Christians if the stories are drawn from the pilgrimages of those who have gone before us in faith and finished the course. For these persons bear testimony to us concerning the One of whom it is written, "Surely he has borne our griefs / and carried our sorrows" (Isa. 53:4 RSV). Their stories point us to his story. And it is his story that enables us to bear all sorrow, for the joy that is set before us through him. His story is the sole source and focus of the entire liturgical calendar.

This book began by recounting Terry Waite's anxiety when, in an underground prison, he feared the loss of sanity because he could not calculate the time of day. But he came to want to know more than the daily schedule of sunset and sunrise. He grew to yearn to observe the cycles of the church, in which he had been nurtured for decades. After nearly three years in solitary confinement, Waite was brought a box of books. It was a jumbled lot of volumes his captors had assembled, seemingly in a most haphazard fashion. But to his great delight the hostage found there a copy of the *Book of Common Prayer*. With great joy he recorded his reaction: "The Prayer Book is invaluable. . . . It helps me give a greater structure to my life. Now I can live the liturgical year."[8]

The sacred calendar is no magical formula; it cannot protect us from all spiritual dryness and misdirection. Nevertheless, this calendar enables us to live—and to die—more readily as the people of God. By observing Christ's time for the church, year in and year out, we make our pilgrim journey—not as if walking in circles on the same plot of ground, but as if ascending a spiral staircase. Annually we go around in what may seem at first to be the same pattern; but gradually it dawns on us that always we see where we have been from a greater height, and by virtue of the increasing elevation we can look farther across the landscape of faith to gain a better perspective on God's gracious design and on our place within it. Thereby we come to believe more confidently, Lord's Day by Lord's Day and Pasch by Pasch, that we, too, will be numbered with the saints in glory everlasting.

EPILOGUE

So what can we make now of the concluding scene of *Places in the Heart?* First, it is crucial that the strange events portrayed occur in the midst of the reception of the Supper of the Lord. It is in the *anamnesis* of Jesus that egregious sinners are transformed, that enemies are reconciled, that the living and the dead dwell together, and that the slayer and the slain are at peace. This *anamnesis* is conjoined with *prolepsis:* This is not simply a congregation in Waxahachie, Texas, in 1935. This is the faithful remembrance of Jesus' death and resurrection, which becomes separated only by the thin moving edge we call the present.

Since earliest Christian times it has been accepted that to attend divine worship is to enter into heaven by anticipation. That is why ancient churches were domed; the dome represented the vault of heaven, and within it (as to this very day among the Orthodox) was the great icon of Christ as Pantocrator: the Almighty ruler of all things. So also, upon entering an Orthodox church, the worshiper is presented with icons of the saints, to be greeted with reverence: To go to church is to encounter the saints as a living reality, no matter how dead they may be regarded as being by an unbelieving world bent on "being realistic."

In the West, modes of representation changed across centuries, but the basic affirmation was retained: To go to church is to go to heaven. In the Middle Ages, when entering the great portals of the house of prayer, the worshiper was greeted by statues of the saints, hovering at eye level or slightly above. Inside, the ceiling was painted blue, embossed with golden stars—the firmament of heaven. The surrounding stained glass, far from being decorative, was to be seen as the colorful stones described in the penultimate chapter of Revelation: jasper, sapphire, agate, emerald, onyx, carnelian, chrysolite, beryl, topaz, chrysoprase, jacinth, and amethyst. The soft, colorful aura produced by the glass represented the distinctive, gracious light of God, which in heaven displaces the more familiar but glaring light of the sun. When the Gothic forms gave way to the Renaissance and Baroque styles, the church ceilings were painted with heavenly scenes: angels, saints, and sometimes the very throne

153

of God. As late as the mosaics added in Victorian times to St. Paul's Cathedral, London, the pictoral theme is Christ in majesty surrounded by the hosts of heaven.

None of this, of course, could be found in rural Texas Protestantism in the 1930s. But there, hymnody supplied what the architecture lacked. It is not unimportant that at the beginning of *Places in the Heart*, and again as the worship service begins at the close of the film, the congregation is singing "Blessed assurance, Jesus is mine! O what a foretaste of glory divine." To enter the church is to enter heaven proleptically, even if that way of stating it would leave the hymn writer (Fanny Crosby) somewhat puzzled.

At the distribution of the sacrament, the hymn being sung by the Waxahachie choir is "In the Garden." Here is a brilliant juxtaposition of themes. As the sacrament is beginning to be shared, the pastor reads words concerning Holy Thursday: "On the night before his crucifixion, our Lord gathered with his disciples. He broke bread and blessed it, saying, 'Take, eat; this is my body.' And he took the cup and said, 'Drink; this is my blood which I shed for thee.'" But all the while the choir is singing, "And he walks with me, and he talks with me, and he tells me I am his own"—a text that its author intended to be understood as Mary Magdalene's joyful song about her Risen Lord on resurrection morning. Thus the anamnesis of Calvary and Easter Day are conjoined, even as anamnesis and prolepsis become one experience.

The events depicted at the movie's end are, in reality, events that lie in the future, and yet powerfully affect the present. For until the future in its incredible strangeness is envisioned, we cannot move toward it or be transformed by its radical newness. Indeed, until the future is envisioned, there can be no dissatisfaction with the present, no prophetic judgment upon its errors or excesses. Far from being "pie in the sky when we die by and by," for the Christian the future is the model for the present: "Your will be done, on earth as in heaven." Therefore it is the perpetual ministry of the humiliated and exalted One to pull past, present, and future into one unified experience for the sake of the church—and, through the ministry of the church, for the sake of the world, which God so eagerly yearns to make perfect.

154

APPENDIX 1

Putting Liturgical Colors in Their Place

For centuries certain vestments worn by clergy and other fabrics used in worship (hangings on or behind the Lord's Table, or at the pulpit and lectern in particular) have been changed according to the liturgical occasion; these changes have followed one or another system of indicating the liturgical season by the alternation of colors.

For generations in both Roman Catholicism and later in Protestant circles, basically four colors were used. White was displayed for the seasons of Christmas and Easter and certain other festival days. Violet (or purple) was used for the preparatory seasons of Advent and Lent (and three pre-Lenten Sundays, in some traditions). Red was used at least for the Day of Pentecost and in some churches for the Sundays thereafter in what we now call "Ordinary Time." Red was also used for days commemorating martyrs. Green was employed when none of the above was assigned, and often it was the color designated for the time between Trinity Sunday and the beginning of Advent, as well as the time between Epiphany and the start of Lent (or pre-Lent). There were slight variations: Black could be used for Good Friday; and on the Third Sunday of Advent and the Fourth Sunday in Lent, rose-colored fabrics were used by some. All of this followed a pattern used in Rome and made generally applicable in Catholicism as a result of the Council of Trent in the sixteenth century; for most of the centuries since, no one questioned the procedure. Many Protestants simply ignored the entire system until a few decades ago; then those who adopted it did so largely without knowing that such a strict codification was a sixteenth-century novelty.

Before the Council of Trent (which overreacted to the Reformation by codifying everything in sight, lest another Luther make undue use of existing latitude), the systems of colors varied widely from place to place. Indeed, in earlier practice color had less to do with legislated use of a particular hue than with the quality of the fabric itself. Often all vestments and hangings were categorized as "the best," "the second best," or "the ordinary"; in the diocese of Sarum in southern England there was indeed the category of "the shabby"! "The best" was for Christmas and Easter, regardless of color, and the ranking proceeded from there downward. Nor was the basic four-color system in force everywhere. English churches often used three colors: red, white, and blue. So open were the rules that before Trent, on Ascension Day "the best" was used in Salisbury; white in Westminster, England; blue in the College of St. Bernard at Romans, France; yellow in Prague; red in Utrecht; and green in Soissons.[1] The existence of such variety and relativity makes it difficult to set down legalistic codes and demand adherence to them on the basis of "ancient catholic precedent."

Furthermore, the standard post-Reformation Western use became very problematical under changing circumstances. Missionaries in Asia were confronted by the fact that white, interpreted as a sign of joy in Europe, connoted mourning in many

155

Eastern cultures. Other cultural complications have arisen; today among certain groups, white is rejected as being an evidence of subtle white racism and thus of discrimination against persons of darker skin.

Nor can undue reliance be placed on the inherent symbolism of colors. Crimson may indeed be reminiscent of blood, and hence be associated with martyrs. On the other hand, the notion that green signifies growth can be misleading; are we to grow in faith only during seasons when green is used? In truth, in the past green was simply what, in the world of computers, is called the default option: Use green when there is no compelling rationale for using something else. Or again, purple (or violet) may have signified royalty in days when purple dye was extremely expensive. But purple is no longer costly, nor do most nations now operate under monarchies. The relativity of color symbolism is further revealed by the fact that violet also has often been said to symbolize penitence, something quite unrelated to its supposed regal connotation.

Suffice it to say that in the context of worship the alternation of colors (as of other visual accoutrements) can be an effective signal to the congregation that now we have entered into a new season or are celebrating a day of special significance. The importance of visual experience in the house of prayer is by no means to be underestimated. But beyond that it is difficult, even perilous, to be rigidly prescriptive.

In the past quarter-century options have multiplied. Because violet presumably connotes penitence, and Advent is now seen as nonpenitential (or less penitential than previously), the alternative use of blue during Advent has gained popularity recently. Gold may be used instead of white for Christmas Day and Easter Day (or for the week following, or for the first forty-nine of the Great Fifty Days, depending on whose suggestions are to be followed). It is even sometimes proposed that two shades of red are needed: fire red (with an orange cast) for Pentecost, and blood red (with a blue cast) to commemorate the martyrs and the passion of Jesus; for red, not violet, is now the color during Holy Week in some churches. It is not difficult to become skeptical about whether the proliferation of colors arises from the needs of the faithful to have the occasion signaled visually or from the desire of the vestment manufacturers to sell more ecclesiastical goods.

In any event, this discussion is placed in an appendix as an indication that while the alternation of colors is not unimportant, the choice of colors is a quite secondary matter, and is far from being the driving force of the liturgical calendar. Theology precedes and interacts with decisions about appropriate colors. Denominations that widely employ colors publish detailed annual guides concerning appropriate use; these publications should be consulted by their congregations. All that can be reported here is a general summary of current practices, as follows.

Advent: Violet (purple) or blue
Christmas: Gold or white for December 24-25. White thereafter, through the Baptism of the Lord. (Or, in the days between January 6 and the Sunday of the Baptism, green may be used.)
Ordinary Time (both after Epiphany-Baptism and after Pentecost): Green
Transfiguration: White
Lent Prior to Holy Week: Violet. Black is sometimes used for Ash Wednesday.
Early Holy Week: On Palm-Passion Sunday, violet (purple) or [blood] red may be specified. For the Monday, Tuesday, and Wednesday of Holy Week, the same options exist, although with variations as to which color to use on each day.

Triduum: For Holy Thursday, violet (purple) or [blood] red may be used during the day and changed to white for the evening Eucharist. Then the church may be stripped.

Good Friday and Holy Saturday: Stripped or black; or [blood] red in some churches on Good Friday.

Great Fifty Days: White or gold. Or gold for Easter Day and perhaps its octave, then white for the remainder of the season until the Vigil of Pentecost.

Day of Pentecost: [Fire] red

Annunciation, Visitation, and Presentation of Jesus: White

Commemoration of Martyrs: [Blood] red

Commemoration of Saints not Martyred: White

All Saints: White

Christ the King: White

APPENDIX 2

Forgetting What You Were Always Taught
(or, This Book in a Nutshell)

For easy reference, prevailing ideas that now are being challenged appear in the left column. The more useful corollaries are in the right column. Numbers in parentheses indicate in which chapter the pertinent information can be found.

If you were taught this:	*Consider instead this:*
The liturgical year begins on the First Sunday of Advent.	Theologically the year begins with Easter (3); chronologically, starting points vary from Eastern to Western churches (6, n. 1).
Advent is primarily about the past expectation of the coming of Messiah.	Advent is primarily about the future, with implications for the present (6).
Christmas is primarily about the birth of the child of Bethlehem.	Christmas is primarily about the great exchange of divinity and humanity in the incarnation and in human sanctification (5).
Christmas is December 25, but Christmas Sunday precedes this when December 25 is not on Sunday.	Christmas is a season, not a day, that begins at sunset on December 24. If December 25 is not on a Sunday, the Sunday following may be designated as "Christmas Sunday" (5).
Epiphany is primarily about the Magi.	Epiphany and the Sunday of the Baptism of the Lord primarily establish the messianic identity of the child of Bethlehem (5).
Epiphany begins a new season that lasts until Lent.	Although interpretations differ, Epiphany can be seen as integral to Christmas, which is followed by "Ordinary Time" (5, 7).

If you were taught this:	*Consider instead this:*
Lent is a sustained consideration of the suffering and death of Jesus.	Lent, until its final week, is a time of disciplined consideration of our life and death as transformed by our covenant with God and is closely related to the administration and reaffirmation of baptism at Easter (4).
The second Sunday before Easter is "Passion Sunday." The Sunday before Easter (Palm Sunday) is a joyous celebration of "the triumphal entry" of Jesus into Jerusalem.	The Sunday before Easter is Palm-Passion Sunday, which sees Jesus' welcome as irony rather than triumph and turns quickly to the story of the passion and crucifixion, which is its principal theme (4).
Holy Thursday evening is a mournful remembrance of Jesus' farewell meal.	The Eucharist on Holy Thursday is the strengthening table prepared in the midst of enemies; it may be preceded by footwashing and followed by the stripping of the chancel (4).
Good Friday is the occasion for interpreting "the seven last words from the cross."	Good Friday is the church's primary day of intercession for the world. The reading of John's passion narrative (in which Jesus speaks only three times) is a proclamation of the divine culmination of an eternal purpose that cannot be defeated by human sin (4).
Easter Day begins with a "sunrise service," held out-of-doors, weather permitting.	The first service of Easter is the Great Vigil, begun in darkness; it includes the service of light, the service of the Word, Baptism, and a festival Eucharist (3, 4).
The Holy Week services on Thursday, Friday, and Sunday morning are separate observances.	The rites at the close of Holy Week constitute a single, extended (though interrupted) service known as "the Triduum" (4).
Easter is a day.	Easter is a season of fifty days (3).
Easter is the primary day of the Christian calendar. "Every Sunday is a little Easter."	Sunday is the primary day of the Christian calendar, from which the season of Easter is derived and upon which it expands. "Every Easter is a Great Sunday" (2, 3).

If you were taught this:	*Consider instead this:*
"Resurrection" refers to the resuscitation of the corpse of Jesus.	The resurrection of the Lord is about far more (not less) than resuscitation. It affirms a cosmic transformation we cannot grasp by human thought or words (1).
The ascension, an event separate from the resurrection, is about the relocation of the revived body of Jesus.	The ascension is a contemplation and elaboration of the meaning of resurrection and has complex theological values that are diminished by a focus on "relocation" (3).
The Day of Pentecost marks the beginning of a new liturgical season.	The Day of Pentecost closes the Great Fifty Days; beyond it extends "Ordinary Time" (3, 7).
The Day of Pentecost marks the beginning of the work of the Spirit in the world.	The Spirit has ever been at work in the world. The Day of Pentecost marks the birth of the church (3).
The Day of Pentecost is primarily about the work of the Spirit in the hearts of individuals.	The Day of Pentecost is primarily about the formation of the church by the Spirit and the mission task thereby given to that corporate body of believers (3).
Trinity Sunday marks the completion of the coming of the Trinity.	The Trinity did not come into being by degrees or in stages; Trinity Sunday recalls the fullness of God's being and work (7).
Transfiguration falls on August 6.	In many current calendars, Transfiguration Sunday, just prior to Lent, sounds important theological themes related to the opening of Lent (7).
"Ordinary Time" means that certain times of the calendar are uneventful.	"Ordinary" refers to a way of counting time (first, second, third . . .) and is not a value judgment about meaning (7).
The commemoration of the saints is alien to most Protestants.	Many Protestants commemorate the saints by naming their congregations after persons in the Bible or denominational founders (8).

If you were taught this:	*Consider instead this:*
All Saints Day is a glorification of great human achievement by ordinary folk.	All Saints Day is a thanksgiving for the grace and power of the risen Christ at work in ordinary folk (8).
Liturgical colors are of primary importance.	Although they may play an important role, liturgical colors are of secondary value in relation to the meaning of the observances to which they are related (Appendix 1).
The use of four liturgical colors is well established and firmly fixed by tradition.	Great variety exists both as to the number and use of colors, both throughout history and currently; often adaptations need to be made due to differing cultural perceptions and symbolic associations (Appendix 1).

161

APPENDIX 3

Calendars
Calendar of Advent-Christmas and Related Dates

Year	First Sunday of Advent	Days of Advent	Day of December 25	Date of Lord's Baptism (next calendar year)	Chanukah begins
1997	Nov. 30	25	Thursday	Jan. 11	Dec. 24
1998	Nov. 29	26	Friday	Jan. 10	Dec. 14
1999	Nov. 28	27	Saturday	Jan. 9	Dec. 4
2000	Dec. 3	22	Monday	Jan. 7	Dec. 22
2001	Dec. 2	23	Tuesday	Jan. 13	Dec. 10
2002	Dec. 1	24	Wednesday	Jan. 12	Nov. 30
2003	Nov. 30	25	Thursday	Jan. 11	Dec. 20
2004	Nov. 28	27	Saturday	Jan. 9	Dec. 8
2005	Nov. 27	28	Sunday	Jan. 8	Dec. 26
2006	Dec. 3	22	Monday	Jan. 7	Dec. 16
2007	Dec. 2	23	Tuesday	Jan. 13	Dec. 5
2008	Nov. 30	25	Thursday	Jan. 11	Dec. 22
2009	Nov. 29	26	Friday	Jan. 10	Dec. 12
2010	Nov. 28	27	Saturday	Jan. 9	Dec. 2
2011	Nov. 27	28	Sunday	Jan. 8	Dec. 21
2012	Dec. 2	23	Tuesday	Jan. 13	Dec. 9
2013	Dec. 1	24	Wednesday	Jan. 12	Nov. 28
2014	Nov. 30	25	Thursday	Jan. 11	Dec. 17
2015	Nov. 29	26	Friday	Jan. 10	Dec. 7
2016	Nov. 27	28	Sunday	Jan. 8	Dec. 25
2017	Dec. 3	22	Monday	Jan. 7	Dec. 13
2018	Dec. 2	23	Tuesday	Jan. 13	Dec. 3
2019	Dec. 1	24	Wednesday	Jan. 12	Dec. 23
2020	Nov. 29	26	Friday	Jan. 10	Dec. 11

Calendar of Lent-Easter and Related Dates

Ash Wednesday	Easter Day	Day of Pentecost	Passover	Orthodox Easter
February 12	March 30	May 18	April 22	April 27
February 25	April 12	May 31	April 11	April 19
February 17	April 4	May 23	April 1	April 11
March 8	April 23	June 11	April 20	April 30
February 28	April 15	June 3	April 8	April 15
February 13	March 31	May 19	March 28	May 5
March 5	April 20	June 8	April 17	April 27
February 25	April 11	May 30	April 6	April 11
February 9	March 27	May 15	April 24	May 1
March 1	April 16	June 4	April 13	April 23
February 21	April 8	May 27	April 3	April 8
February 6	March 23	May 11	April 20	April 27
February 25	April 12	May 31	April 9	April 19
February 17	April 4	May 23	March 30	April 4
March 9	April 24	June 12	April 19	April 24
February 22	April 8	May 27	April 7	April 15
February 13	March 31	May 19	March 26	May 5
March 5	April 20	June 8	April 15	April 20
February 18	April 5	May 24	April 4	April 12
February 10	March 27	May 15	April 23	May 1
March 1	April 16	June 4	April 11	April 16
February 14	April 1	May 20	March 31	April 8
March 6	April 21	June 9	April 20	April 28
February 26	April 12	May 31	April 9	April 19

NOTES

1. Living at the Intersection of Time and Eternity

1. Terry Waite, *Taken on Trust* (New York, San Diego, London: Harcourt Brace & Co., 1993), p. 12.

2. To speak of "God's intervention in history" became popular in the mid–twentieth century, particularly in the movement known as "biblical theology." This is very ironic since at the time of the rise of this way of speaking the two dominant English translations of the scriptures were the King James (Authorized) Version and the Revised Standard Version, neither of which uses the term "intervene" in any of its forms.

3. Adapted with contemporary spelling and punctuation from *The Sermons of John Donne*, edited with introductions, and critical apparatus by Evelyn M. Simpson and George R. Potter, in ten volumes (Berkeley and Los Angeles: University of California Press, 1962). This is Sermon 2 of vol. 7 of the series, p. 249. (In the older *LXXX Sermons of Donne*, it is Sermon no. 4.) Donne was Dean at St. Paul's when he preached this sermon.

4. If we have domesticated the Incarnation to the point that we do not recognize its inherent scandal, we do well to ponder Christian history. In the early centuries a significant number of Christians believed that before the death of Jesus occurred, the divine nature was separated from the human nature and returned to heaven; thus what died was only a physical shell that no longer encased the Holy One of God. It has also been suggested by some that Jesus only seemed to die on the cross; in fact, this theory asserts, Jesus merely fell into a deep coma and later was revived. Both scenarios have been rejected by the church because they sell short what the New Testament is trying to tell us about the deep humiliation of God in Christ.

5. This hymn appears in differing translations in various hymnals. This translation was made in 1931 by Percy Dearmer. Another popular translation is that done earlier by John Mason Neale. Some hymnals use variations of these or some composite text; fortunately in almost all hymnals the hymn is listed under the same title: "Sing, My Tongue, the Glorious Battle," which must not be confused with a eucharistic hymn by Thomas Aquinas usually entitled "Sing, My Tongue, the Savior's Glory."

6. "Holy" in its ancient Hebraic sense does not primarily mean "sanctified" or "righteous" but means "drastically other," "apart from or beyond" the common realms of experience.

7. It is taken for granted among scholars that the Gospels of Luke and John were written later than those of Matthew and Mark. This chronology should not be taken to mean too much, if for no other reason than that all four authors were setting down in writing traditions that had been around for decades, but largely in oral form. Nor should it be assumed that the latter writers had seen the documents

prepared by the earlier writers. Still, chronology does count for something. As Christian communities more and more reflected on the events of Jesus' presence and on their own interpretation of that presence, increasingly they must have wrestled with what "resurrection" means in the instance of Jesus. It is not unlikely that the earliest interpretations had to do largely with resuscitation; in response, some believers may have presented as an alternative a sort of otherworldly existence rather divorced from physical reality. Thus Luke and John seem to address both points, and find both to be inadequate.

8. This passage is difficult to interpret, however. It can mean "do not touch me" in a literal sense, or "do not restrain me" in a figurative sense. Hence not too much weight should be assigned to this piece of data.

9. Let it be noted that no New Testament writer presumes to describe the actual event of the resurrection. Only its effects (the appearances of the Risen One) are reported. This in itself is a testimony to the mysteriousness of the resurrection. No human can report having seen it, heard it, or felt it occur. Later artists who attempted to depict the event itself wisely show the guards at the tomb stunned into unconsciousness. Note also the paucity of visual symbols for the resurrection, and the limitations of those that are used. Sunrises, flowers, and butterflies, lovely though they are, are inadequate as symbols. For once the secrets of astronomy and biology are known these are utterly predictable, the working out of natural forces; but the resurrection is unpredictable and is a sheer gift, not a consequence of anything except divine love. The symbols of resurrection that do work, work largely by negativity: an empty cross, an empty tomb. The exception is the resurrection banner: a pennant with a red cross on a white background, often shown being held by the Risen Christ or by the victorious Lamb of God.

10. Nor should the resurrection be equated with parapsychological states, communication with the dead through seances, or out-of-body and near-death experiences of "another world." Some or all of these may be valid and verifiable through scientific measures not now known to us. They may even be intimations or prefigurings of existence outside our usual perceptions. Still, the resurrection of Jesus lies beyond all of them—not necessarily contradicting them but giving us the barest glimpse of a glory beyond all powers we have to describe. Any literalistic assumptions are idolatrous. It is quite appropriate for scripture to describe God's eternal realm in earthly terms; streets of gold, gates of pearl, beings with six wings, and so on. As human beings we are constrained to give concrete expression to our theology. But to take these things for literal description is to diminish the grandeur of God who has ways past our understanding, who has no need of streets or gates or seraphim. We can no more envision accurately what awaits us than a child in its mother's womb can describe what life will be like after birth. That is indeed one of the implications of Jesus' words to Nicodemus about the birth that comes from above. Theology worth its salt is an imaginative form of discourse that admits straightaway the limits both of language and of imagination; further, such theology does not equate "imagination" with "fabrication" but insists that truth about God requires breaking through the boundaries of ordinary thought. That is why the construction of theology is both so necessary and so perilous. The divine cannot be grasped by ordinary human categories alone; but even our best extraordinary efforts will touch merely the hem of God's outermost garment. In such efforts, however, there is sufficient power to transform.

11. In the United States, this form of the collect is shared with slight variations by the most recent liturgy books of The Episcopal Church, the Inter-Lutheran

bodies, and the joint Presbyterian bodies. This is the collect for the First Sunday after Christmas, except for the Episcopalians, who assign it to the Second Sunday after Christmas (which does not occur when December 25 falls on Sunday, Monday, or Tuesday).

12. United Methodists and some other Wesleyans will recall the language of their familiar eucharistic prayer in traditional language, which contains the petition that we, receiving the gifts of bread and wine, "may be partakers of the divine nature through" the One whose body and blood we partake. This is a twentieth-century addition for Methodists; it may or may not reflect the touted affinity of contemporary Methodist thought with Eastern Orthodox theology, though certainly the East has far more readily talked about "the divinization of humanity" by the grace of the atonement and the resurrection than have most Western Christians.

2. The Year of Our Risen Lord

1. There are several difficulties with these designations. First, there is a linguistic oddity. Until recently, at least, in most Western languages the divisions of time were designated by two Latin terms: *Ante Christum* (meaning "before Christ" and abbreviated A.C.) and *Anno Domini* (properly translated "in the year of the Lord" and abbreviated A.D.). In the English-speaking world, the Latin "A.D." was accepted while "A.C." was replaced with the English phrase "before Christ" (B.C.).

Another difficulty has to do with written style. A year of the pre-Christian era is properly designated "500 A.C. or 500 B.C." (that is, "the 500th year before Christ"). But a year within the Christian era is properly designated "A.D. 500" (that is, "in the 500th year of our Lord" or "in the year of our Lord, the 500th"). As Latin has come to be an alien language among us, one now usually finds instead "500 A.D."; this can accurately be translated only in the nonsensical form of "the 500th in the year of our Lord." Further, since "Anno Domini" means "in the year . . ." it is redundant to write "This happened in the year A.D. 1910" or even "This happened in A.D. 1910." The correct form is "This happened A.D. 1910." But such niceties of style probably are hardly worth the argument any longer.

Of greater import now is the fact that in a multicultural world, persons of other religious traditions (or none) rightly object to having to calculate time on a basis established by adherents of Christianity. Thus the increasingly common designations are "B.C.E." and "C.E." with the years preceding these letters in both cases (500 B.C.E. and 500 C.E.). The designations mean, respectively, "500th year before the common era" and "500th year of the common era." While being able to speak of time without mentioning the name of Christ may make non-Christians more comfortable, in a deeper sense these recent designations solve nothing; for the dividing point between B.C.E. and C.E. is still determined by the timing of Jesus' life and thus perpetuates a Christian cultural dominance. Ultimately some other dividing line or manner of designation may be devised to avoid such hegemony.

Until then, it is wise for Christians to use the new designations when addressing remarks to the general populace. When addressing only other Christians, however, it can still be an important assertion of faith to proclaim that we are living "in the Year of our Lord XXXX." This acknowledges our conviction that by virtue of incarnation, death, and resurrection Jesus Christ has laid claim to and transformed our understanding of time. This dual usage acknowledges (a) that we cannot impose our faith claims on those who prefer not to accept them; (b) that as

Christians we are still bound to confess that Christ has significantly altered our own perceptions of history.

2. Because the term means "seventh," it is not appropriate as a designation for Sunday, which is the first day of the week; nevertheless, Christian groups (particularly the Puritans) have frequently thus misused the word "sabbath" for the first day of the week, and in the process have often imposed on the Lord's Day prohibitions not necessarily appropriate to it—particularly legalistic regulations concerning what kind of work, if any, may be done on the day.

3. The significance of the seventh day evolved within ancient Hebraic practice, as can be seen by comparing the two justifications in the Ten Commandments for its observance. In the older version of the Decalogue (Deut. 5:12-15), the sabbath observance is a perpetual commemoration of the Exodus: "Remember that you were a slave in the land of Egypt, and the LORD your God brought you out from there with a mighty hand and an outstretched arm; therefore the LORD your God commanded you to keep the sabbath day" (Deut. 5:15). But in the later version of the Decalogue, another rationale is given: "For in six days the LORD made heaven and earth, the sea, and all that is in them, but rested the seventh day; therefore the LORD blessed the sabbath day and consecrated it" (Exod. 20:11). This evolution allowed for an expansion of the claims of faith: Only those of Hebraic origin could be expected to observe a holy day on the basis of the exodus, but the entire human race could be asked to observe a day based on the act of creation.

4. Probably the oldest prophetic citation is Amos 5:18-20. See the entry "Day of the Lord" in *Interpreter's Dictionary of the Bible* (Nashville: Abingdon Press, 1962), vol. 1 [A-D], pp. 784-85.

5. Herein is evidence that the ancient theologians of the church did not fall into the trap of a wooden literalism about the length of creation that characterizes some "creationist" approaches of today. The seventh day lasted from the end of creation until the coming of Jesus, and the eighth day extends from the time of Jesus until the fulfillment of the reign of Christ; so from this perspective why should the first six days be understood as periods of only twenty-four hours each?

6. In certain liturgical traditions principal feasts are extended out to the eighth day. Thus the Sunday following Easter Day is called "The Octave of Easter"; and January 1 is the "Octave of Christmas." All eight days embraced by the feast and its octave are times of particular solemnity. While "octave" is derived from a Latin term meaning "eighth," not "eight," in casual usage "octave" often refers to all eight days, not simply to the final day of the observance. Hebraic antecedents for this liturgical character of a closing eighth day are found in Lev. 23:36 and 2 Chron. 7:9.

7. Stanza 2 of the hymn "O Day of Rest and Gladness" by Christopher Wordsworth (1807–85).

8. This phrase is usually translated into English as "Sun of Righteousness." I have elected an alternative form for two reasons. (1) The Hebrew term can be properly translated either way. (2) "Righteousness" has become such a "churchy" word that often we pass it off as religious jargon somewhat disconnected from daily life. As a more secular word, "justice" may confront us more readily with what the scriptures are actually trying to say to us in practical terms.

9. The hymn is no. 728 in the *United Methodist Hymnal* under the title "Come Sunday." It is not coincidental that, amid a general disregard for Sunday as a longing for heaven, this text has come from the crucible of African American suffering. Distressed Christians in any age are more in touch with the weekly

Sunday as a yearning for the eternal Sunday than are comfortable Christians. "Come Sunday" is from *Black, Brown & Beige* by Duke Ellington. Copyright © 1946 (Renewed) by G. Schirmer, Inc. (ASCAP) International Copyright Secured. All Rights Reserved. Reprinted by Permission.

10. In those churches that observe Christmas with services on the evening of December 24 but not on December 25, an interesting phenomenon occurs when December 25 falls on a Sunday. Debates arise as to whether or not the usual Sunday service should be held, as if the Lord's Day were a dispensable occasion simply because Christmas Day in these circles has become a domestic occasion rather than a liturgical one. I once knew a pastor who refused to conduct worship on Sunday, December 25. His rationale: "That is my day to be home with my family." But no! The ancient witness of the church is that every Sunday is the Lord's Day, not our day to do with as we will.

11. The term "office" has developed from the Latin word *officium,* meaning service; it originally had connotations of obligation. The "daily office" was a pattern of worship Christians were obliged to observe each day in their service to God. The liturgies were also known as "the office hours," because set hours of the day were designated for their observance. Unfortunately, later usage of this phrase in the business world makes the term now either amusing or confusing. Thus today "the office hours" are often referred to as "the liturgy of the hours." An alternative term for "daily office" is "divine office."

In the full monastic tradition the office hours were Nocturns and Lauds (often combined and in medieval times said in the middle of the night, though originally Lauds was said at daybreak); Prime (upon arising); Terce (at nine in the morning); Sext (noon); None (at three in the afternoon); Vespers (at sunset); and Compline (immediately before retiring). Exact timing varied, however, particularly from summer to winter and from south to north, corresponding to the great variations in the length of daylight across Europe. When Nocturns and Lauds are counted separately, the hours number eight, a number whose symbolism we have just discussed. When the two services are combined, the hours number seven; often this way of counting was justified by appealing to Psalm 119:164: "Seven times a day I praise you."

At the Reformation in England, Archbishop Thomas Cranmer collated the various rites and reduced their number to two, thereby reinventing the morning and evening prayer service of the ancient cathedrals. Lutherans on the continent followed a similar practice.

12. Stanzas 2 and 3 of John Ellerton's "The Day Thou Gavest, Lord, Is Ended."

13. Although this suggestion is intended for all, it is particularly pertinent to clergy and other church professionals for whom Sunday is a "workday." Those of us who fit this category tend to bemoan the fact that we ourselves have such a hectic Sunday pace, often to our spiritual detriment. I can attest personally to the great benefit I have discovered in making Saturday evening the beginning of my Lord's Day observance. Such a revised perception is more practical for those who, because of Sunday duties, accept very few Saturday evening social obligations and can readily adapt to this way of calculating time. It does mean that those Sunday preparations that are regarded as "work" (finishing the sermon, practicing the organ voluntary, and so on) need to be completed before Saturday evening arrives. On the other hand, such a revised calculating of time is very difficult where the increasing popularity of Saturday evening services of worship is operative.

Rightly motivated, the move to a Saturday evening service can be in its own way a reorientation of Christian time. It will not solve the problem of the schedule of the pastor, church musician, or other persons who plan and conduct the services. But it can be a way of asserting that Christians reckon the day from evening to evening. Usually, however, a quite different motivation is at work. Services are scheduled on Saturday evening primarily for the convenience of those who attend them, so they can have the whole of the next day to do something else. When the time of weekly worship is determined by human convenience rather than theological affirmation, trouble lies ahead. Soon it will be asked, "Why not abandon Saturday evening and Sunday entirely as worship times (so we can have a full weekend unencumbered by such "distractions") and have the weekly service on Thursday evening?" There goes the Lord's Day and everything it has signified ever since the founding of the church. Those congregations desiring Saturday evening worship services are well advised to see them as the beginning of Sunday, even if they precede actual sunset.

But the ambiguous line between scheduling Saturday evening services out of historical and theological conviction versus out of sheer convenience will not go away. The Roman Church provides Saturday evening masses and, in line with ancient usage, calls them "vigil masses," thereby indicating that they belong to Sunday's activities. Still, that church in its legislation waffles on the matter by saying that Saturday evening and other holy-day masses may begin before sunset except at Easter, when there must be a true vigil mass that begins no earlier than sunset and preferably after dusk. Such compromises will be unavoidable by the rest of us.

3. Easter: The Great Fifty Days

1. Recent attempts to relate the word "Easter" to Christian roots rather than to the Teutonic goddess seem unconvincing to me. However that may be, in English and German the respective terms (Easter and Ostern) connote "east"—the direction in which to look for the rising of the sun. We have noted in chapter 2 how the ancient church used to its theological advantage language about the sun. But directional language also had a theological role. On the basis of Matthew 24:27 ("As the lightning comes from the east and flashes as far as the west, so will be the coming of the Son of Man"), it was believed that on the final day the Lord would appear in glory in the east—the dawn of the eternal reign of the Sun of Justice. Further, the west was deemed to be the domain of the devil. Hence this lightning flashing as far as the west would illumine (and thus dissipate) the nature of evil. On the positive side, it is to be said all of this affirms the eschatological character of the resurrection; on the negative side, it must be admitted that Christians today attending an Easter sunrise service make no such eschatological associations and probably would deem a bit odd any preacher who on that occasion tried to do so.

2. It is often erroneously suggested that "Pasch" is derived from the Greek word *paschein*, meaning to suffer; on that basis, it is supposed "Pasch" refers to the suffering of Jesus. In fact the word is derived from the Hebrew *pesach*, which is correctly translated as "Passover." *Pesach* came into both Greek and Latin as *Pascha*, a form that in English can be used interchangeably with "Pasch." The confusion in derivation goes back to the Christian writers of the second and third centuries, most of whom knew little or no Hebrew; because of the esteem in which those writers are held, their error is accepted as truth and perpetuated by many who quote their works.

3. See, for example: George Hugh Bourne's "Lord, enthroned in heavenly splendor" ("Paschal Lamb, thine offering"); Robert Campbell's "At the Lamb's high

169

feast" ("Where the Paschal blood is poured" and "Paschal victim, Paschal bread"); John Blackwell and Martin Madam's "Hail, thou once despised Jesus" ("Paschal Lamb, by God appointed"); John Mason Neale's translation from the Latin, "The Lamb's high banquet" ("Protected in the Paschal night"); Catherine Winkworth's translation of a Michael Weisse text, "Christ the Lord is risen again" ("Christ, our Paschal Lamb indeed"); and a text attributed to Wypo of Burgundy entitled "Christians, to the Paschal Victim." See also some translations of Luther's "Christ Jesus lay in death's strong bands" ("Here the true Paschal Lamb we see").

4. Among earliest Christians, some calculated Easter on the basis of the chronology of John's Gospel, which indicated Jesus died on the day of Preparation of Passover. But others followed the Synoptic chronologies, which suggest that Jesus died on the afternoon before. To add to the confusion, before the dating of Easter was set, a debate raged within the church concerning the appropriate day of the week for the observance. The prevailing party argued that the annual festival must always begin on a Sunday: The annual Great Easter Day must coincide with the weekly Lord's Day. The losing party, dubbed the "Quartodecimans" (meaning fourteenth), argued that the timing of Easter Day should be determined in relation to the fourteenth day of the Jewish lunar month Nisan, by which the date of Passover is fixed in Judaism; but that would have meant the Christian Pasch could fall on any day of the week, and only rarely on a Sunday. To make certain that the Quartodecimans got not even the smallest concession, the prevailing party decreed that in those years when the date of Passover and Sunday do coincide, Easter Day must be moved from that Sunday to the next Lord's Day.

The general rule for the dating of Easter is this: Easter Day is the first Sunday after the first full moon that falls on or after March 21, while never coinciding with the Jewish dating of Passover. Reliable sources will say not "March 21" but "the spring equinox." They are technically correct with regard to the legislation established at the Council of Nicea, A.D. 325; but there is one further wrinkle. For ecclesiastical purposes the time of the full moon is determined not by modern astronomy but by old astronomical tables that are slightly out of kilter. In true astronomy the equinox will vary with the latitude and can fall before March 21, but according to these old tables it cannot. For Western Christians (Catholics and Protestants), Easter Day can fall on any date between March 22 and April 25, inclusive. Just to make life more perplexing, the Eastern churches (Greek Orthodox, Russian Orthodox, and so on), also follow the ruling of Nicea but use yet a more antiquated set of astronomical tables based on the older Julian calendar, rather than the Gregorian calendar of the West. Therefore, Orthodox Easter never precedes Western Easter (despite what some encyclopedias say); usually it lags behind by one, four, or five weeks and can fall into early May.

Setting a fixed date for Easter Day has often been advocated to no avail. Indeed the Second Vatican Council of the Roman Church declared it saw no impediment to a fixed date, provided all Christians would concur. Rome even proposed that beginning in 1977 Easter Day be uniformly observed on the day after the second Saturday of April. This admirable proposal died, apparently for lack of interest among the Orthodox and Protestants. (One can imagine murmurings of "But we've never done it that way before," and surmise a deep-seated reluctance to do anything suggested by the pope.)

5. Anti-Semitism has deep roots within Christianity. From the second century on, we can find in Christian writing diatribes against Judaism that should be of great embarrassment to us. Even more pressing is the view of some scholars that

anti-Semitism is embedded in the Fourth Gospel. Other interpreters assert that John is not characterizing all Jews in passages such as 5:18 and 8:22, but is referring to one particular point of view within some Jewish communities of his day, and that it is only our own anti-Semitism read back into the Fourth Gospel that creates a misimpression. In support of this interpretation is an otherwise very puzzling passage in 13:33 in which Jesus says, "As I said to the Jews so now I say to you." If "the Jews" were all Jews, Jesus would here have to be talking to Gentiles; but he is, in fact, addressing his Jewish followers.

The trickiness of generic versus specific language may be illustrated by pointing out that all citizens of the U.S.A. can generically be called "republicans" because the United States is a republic. Or with equal truth, all U.S. citizens can be called "democrats" by virtue of living in a democracy. But more commonly those two labels have restricted meanings that denote a specific division of opinion regarding internal policies of this democratic republic. Were it not for capitalization, it could be difficult to know which meaning is intended, the generic or the specific. Since ancient manuscripts normally did not use a different form of letter at the beginning of a proper name, interpretation can be difficult.

It is crucial to remember two things: (1) Jesus and all of his followers were Jews, as were all of the early converts to the apostolic faith. The assertion of Paul that the gospel should be taken to the Gentiles resulted in such a furor that a church council had to be convened to discuss Paul's ministry and its implications for practices such as circumcision and dietary laws (Acts 15). Even after the council, some of the apostles had difficulty conforming to its decision (see Gal. 2). (2) When blatant anti-Semitism arises, it is within a Christianity that has become thoroughly Gentile in its ethnic origins. Thus anti-Semitism is imported into Christianity as prejudicial baggage from long-standing cultural animosities between Jews and Gentiles. This animosity indeed is already evident in the letter of Paul, a Jew, to the largely Gentile church at Rome. There Paul asserts, particularly in chapters 9–11, the continuity of Judaism and Christianity and seems to do this because he knows that continuity is under dispute in Rome even in the late first century.

The popularization of the term "Pasch" is not a quick remedy to anti-Semitism. Although its use can be interpreted in the way set forth in the main text of this chapter, the term can and often has been used in quite the opposite sense to assert that Christ is the true and only Passover of God, and that the antecedent practices of the Jews were mere shadows of things to come, which have now been overthrown and made obsolete by the real thing. Unhappily, that view feeds anti-Semitism to an alarming degree.

6. The term *pentekoste* is Greek meaning fiftieth. Among Hellenistic Jews it was the translation into their native tongue of the Hebrew term translated into English as "Feast of Weeks" (see Deut. 16:9-12). On the second day (16 Nisan) after the beginning of Passover the spring barley harvest was ritualistically begun. Fifty days later the completion of the subsequent wheat harvest was signaled with great celebration. But *pentekoste* can be a generic term for the entire fifty-day period of harvest as well as a specific term for the final day. In Acts 2, the latter use is intended. However, in both ancient synagogue and church the entire period was often referred to as "the Pentecost." This ambiguity can cause great confusion when reading the related literature.

7. It is sometimes said erroneously that the seven-day week is based on a lunar calendar. But a lunar month consists of 29.5 days and is more readily divided into three ten-day periods (as in the calendars of the Greeks) than into four seven-day

periods with 2.5 days left over. The seven-day week had its origins in the Middle East before the rise of Judaism; and among the Jews, at least, its justification came to be theological, not astronomical.

8. Kneeling for communion, so familiar to the Western churches, is a relatively late custom and one never adopted by the Eastern churches where communion is always received in a standing position for the reason given above. In the West, during the Middle Ages theologians pondered the implications of court etiquette for worship. "We kneel when we enter the throne room of an earthly monarch," they reasoned; "so how much more should such respect be shown when at the Eucharist we approach the courts of heaven." History has provided us with an interesting corollary. In most democracies it is unthinkable that citizens should kneel out of respect for the head of state; yet when a head of state walks into a room of seated people, almost involuntarily everyone rises—with one very significant exception: in church (or other religious setting), wherein a head of state is a worshiper on a par with everyone else and wherein standing is a mark of honor reserved to God.

9. Philip T. Weller, ed. and trans., *Selected Easter Sermons of St. Augustine* (St. Louis: B. Herder Book Co., 1959), p. 124.

10. In English-speaking countries the second Sunday of Easter has been referred to in the past as "Low Sunday." Such reference is best discontinued. No one knows for certain why it was called that. Often days were popularly called by titles derived from a poor grasp of Latin texts assigned for the day. Since forms of the word "laudo" (Latin for "to praise") were used frequently on this day, it may be that what the educated called "Laudo Sunday" was perceived before the Reformation by the non–Latin-speaking populace as "Low Sunday." Others give the origin of the term "Low Sunday" a psychological twist: In contrast to the great celebration of Easter Day itself, the services a week later are by comparison a let-down; and then there were all of the bad jokes about "Low Sunday" referring to the poor attendance in comparison to that a week earlier. The old designation deserves to be abandoned in favor of a title that has clear meaning.

11. From "O Sons and Daughters, Let Us Sing," John Mason Neale's translation of a fifteenth-century text by Jean Tisserand. For slight variations of format as to how the hymn is to be used on two consecutive Sundays, see the most recent hymnals of the Episcopalians, Presbyterians, and United Methodists.

12. No. 29 in the collection of the 166 eucharistic hymns published in 1745 by John and Charles Wesley. The text can readily be sung to a variety of Common Meter tunes, including one no English-speaking congregation can claim not to know: "Amazing Grace." Stanza 2 originally began "Of thee we commune still," but the slightly revised text quoted here has become standard because the accents of the syllables flow more readily with most tunes.

13. This assertion is made in part at least on grammatical grounds. In most languages the present-tense verb that accompanies "I" is used for no other pronoun. Therefore in many languages (though oddly, not English) it is deemed unnecessary to say "I am." "Am" alone conveys all the necessary information. Even English-speaking children know this instinctively. "Am going outside, Daddy," says the child. "No, Dear" replies the parent, ever eager to inculcate good grammar, "*I* am going outside." "Oh?" comes the response. "Are you going with me?" Greek was more economical; unless there was some reason to stress the role of speaker, "I" (*ego*) was omitted in favor of a simple "am" (*eimi*). When the *ego* is included, the alert reader pays attention and asks why. And in every instance of Jesus' "I am"

172

sayings in John, the full *ego eimi* is used. The reason may well be to call to mind the "I AM" of Exodus 3.

14. From the hymn text "What Wondrous Love Is This, O My Soul?" published at least as early as 1811.

15. The name of God that lies behind the words "I AM" is usually transliterated into English as YHWH but, following Jewish practice, is not translated. In older translations it was brought into English as "Jehovah," a form now known to have been inaccurate. More recent English versions (The *Jerusalem Bible* being an exception) further follow Judaic tradition by not printing out in the translation YHWH in any form; instead, the English translation of another Hebrew name for God, *Adonai* ("Lord"), is substituted. In some recent translations of the Hebrew Scriptures (including both the RSV and the NRSV), the Hebrew name can readily be determined even in translation. If the normal style of type is used (Lord), the Hebrew term being translated is *Adonai*. But when the word appears in all uppercase letters, with the first letter being larger (LORD), the Hebrew term YHWH underlies the English text.

The Hebraic tension between familiar names for God and the most Holy Name that is never to be uttered may find expression in the best known of all biblical prayers. "Our Father" at the beginning of the Lord's Prayer may well grow out of the most familiar title a child could use for a male parent in Jesus' culture: *abba*, the Aramaic equivalent of "daddy." (See Mark 14:36, Romans 8:15, and Galatians 4:6 in which the authors in each case use the untranslated Aramaic term, and then translate it into Greek, from which it is translated into English, perhaps too formally, as "father.") The "hallowed be your Name," following the opening address, may well allude to that Most Holy Name of God, which is never to cross the lips of the faithful—YHWH—for which *Adonai* is always substituted. If this is a viable interpretation of the Lord's Prayer, it should be a powerful indication to Christians that we are called upon to maintain a vital balance between a close personal familiarity with God and an awestruck silence.

16. The evidences of this unity are in the New Testament itself. In the shorter ending of Mark's Gospel, no ascension is mentioned. In the longer ending (16:9-20), the ascension seems to occur on the evening of (as we would say) or the evening following (counting sunset to sunset) resurrection day. Jesus appears to Magdalene, then to the two at Emmaus, then to the eleven, and then is taken into heaven, all within the space of a few hours. If it seems otherwise to us, it is because we impose upon Mark the chronology of the Acts. The same imposition causes us to read Matthew 28:16-20 as an ascension narrative, in which case there is a space of days (though a number is not specified) between resurrection and ascension, since the disciples must journey from Jerusalem to Galilee. But in fact Matthew says nothing whatever about an ascension. His chronology can be read to mean that what happened in Galilee is a post-ascension appearance. In John's Gospel there is also no reported ascension, and again the appearance to the eleven can as easily be interpreted as post-ascension. John does allude to the ascension when Jesus asks Magdalene not to touch him (20:17) but gives neither a narrative nor a chronology. It is plausible that John assumed the ascension occurred shortly after the appearance to Magdalene, and that the evening appearances to the eleven in chapter 20 are post-ascension events.

The establishment of a clear ascension chronology thus falls to Luke. But even here we have to question our standard assumption that "of course Luke puts the ascension on the fortieth day." In the second of his two-volume work, Luke speaks of Jesus appearing to the apostles "during forty days" (Acts 1:3); but even the chronological location of verses 6-11 is not specific concerning a fortieth day. Of greater importance is that in his Gospel, Luke seems to be quite in accord with the other Gospels; when Luke 24 is read without the "forty days" reference of Acts in mind, an unprejudiced eye will conclude that on the evening after the resurrection Jesus appeared at Emmaus and amid the followers in Jerusalem, immediately after which the assembled company walked to Bethany where Jesus bade them farewell and was taken into heaven.

In conclusion then, the placement of the ascension celebration on the fortieth day is a late addition of the original Christian calendar, and hangs entirely on one phrase in the Acts, which in itself is ambiguous. What may be far more important than the literal meaning of "during forty days" is its symbolic meaning. In the Hebrew tradition, (whether it be forty years in the wilderness as in the case of ancient Israel, the forty days of rain in the time of Noah, the forty days of Moses at Mt. Sinai, or the forty days of Elijah or Jesus in the wilderness) forty connotes a fullness of time, a completeness of activity. Thus the Risen Lord is with the disciples for as long as necessary in order to accomplish what needs to be done, whether that happens to be 960 hours or some other number.

17. All of this is precisely the underpinning of the phrase so many Christians find disconcerting while saying the Apostles' Creed: "He descended to the dead" (or "into hell," to use the older and even more puzzling phraseology). This creedal assertion means far more than that Christ truly died; it means that even in death Christ was effecting salvation for imprisoned humanity, giving life to dead spirits. Even crucifixion cannot keep God from being gracious!

18. This text as it is given here appears in the *United Methodist Hymnal*. Since the publication of that book in 1989, Wren has revised the text several times. An intermediate revision appears in the *Presbyterian Hymnal*; a still later form of the text is found in Wren's *Faith Renewed* (Carol Stream, Ill.: Hope Publishing Co., 1995). The revisions, according to Wren, were made to change the focus of the text somewhat, not because of doctrinal dissatisfaction with the original version. Because the focus of the original text better illustrates my points about the ascension than do the later versions, Wren has encouraged me to use the earlier version here. © 1975 by Hope Publishing Co. All rights reserved. Used by permission.

19. The opening words of a text by John R. Peacey.

20. In early versions of the three-year lectionary, Genesis 11:1-9 was appointed as the first reading in Year C. Although this has been altered in subsequent revisions, the Babel and Pentecost narratives can still be read in tandem with great effectiveness.

21. The stanzas (and several more) by Charles Wesley appear in hymnals under the title "Come, Sinners, to the Gospel Feast."

22. Although English hymnal versions vary slightly, most (including this) are based on the 1854 translation of Richard Massie. Luther wrote the text in 1524; his text borrows from the medieval hymns "Victimae paschali laudes" and "Surrexit Christus hodie."

4. Lent: Forty Days of Devotion and Discipline

1. Roman Catholics now consider that Lent actually ends on the evening of Holy Thursday, in order that the liturgies of Thursday evening through the Easter Vigil (the Triduum) may be preserved as a unity. According to this reckoning, Lent

consists of thirty-eight weekdays plus six Sundays. But as noted below, "forty" has always been a rounded number of convenience, not a detailed way of counting.

Some but not all liturgical calendars use a different preposition with relation to Lenten Sundays as a way of separating them a bit from the season itself: Sundays "of Advent" and "of Easter," but Sundays "in Lent."

2. The earliest preparation for the Easter Vigil seems to have been a stringent fast of forty hours' duration. By a slow alteration over centuries, forty hours got extended to forty days with the understandable result that an absolute fast from food was greatly relaxed and adapted. In the early centuries the development of extended fasting had a complex history, of which only the final results are considered here. For an account of this development see "Lent" by Lizette Larson-Miller, pp. 680-87 in the *New Dictionary of Sacramental Worship* edited by Peter E. Fink, S.J. (Collegeville, Minn.: Liturgical Press, 1990).

3. In European languages the pre-Easter season is usually designated by its length or by the characteristic of fasting. Thus, Spanish, Italian, and French use titles for the season related to the number forty: *cuaresma, quarésma,* and *carême* respectively. German designates the season in accordance with dietary restraint: *Fastenzeit,* the time of fasting. English is doubly short-changed. Our primary term for the time of resurrection makes no explicit reference to Christ or the Paschal mystery, and our term "Lent" has no spiritual connotations. It is simply an old form of the word "length" and has to do with the lengthening of the hours of daylight as one approaches the vernal equinox. As such, of course, it makes no sense at all in English-speaking countries of the Southern Hemisphere. English-speaking churches may well try to introduce the practice of referring to "the Forty Days," but there is not even the partial precedent for this that we have through the use of "paschal" and "the Great Fifty Days" for the Easter season.

4. Traditionally the ashes are the burned palms from the previous Palm-Passion Sunday, mixed perhaps with olive oil to cause them to cohere. The symbolism is evident: Our joyous acclamations of "Hosanna" wither and die like cut greenery; even our best intentions ultimately require the mercy of a compassionate God. Under no circumstances should wood ash be used; for in addition to lacking the symbolic connotations, under certain conditions wood ash mixed with perspiration can produce a form of lye that results in caustic burns.

5. In Roman Catholic adaptations of the lectionary, the readings for Year A may be used also in Years B and C in any parish where the *Rite of Christian Initiation for Adults* (RCIA) is being used in those years, precisely because of these allusions to baptism.

6. Some years ago in rush-hour traffic I followed a car with a personalized plate that read "TRIDUUM." So poorly known was the word then (even less so than now) that I came up with an elaborate explanation of what it might mean to the owner: Perhaps three [TRI] members of his family belonged to the Delta Upsilon [DU] fraternity at the nearby University of Maryland [UM]. It seemed more plausible than believing the owner of a car far too expensive to belong to a cleric would know anything about the liturgical Triduum. By good fortune, at a red light I was able to roll up alongside the vehicle and get the driver's attention. "Are you by any chance a specialist in liturgy?" I asked. "No," came the reply with obvious puzzlement. "Then excuse the inquiry," I yelled sheepishly. "I am one, and in my field the word on your license plate has a very technical meaning." Just then the traffic signal turned green; but while pulling away, the driver shouted back: "Oh yes. Triduum. It's the same Triduum we're both talking about." Unless some kind reader can put

175

me in touch with the Virginian who owns that tag, I shall have to go to my death wondering how all that came to be! And I always tell my students from Virginia they simply have to know the term "Triduum," if for no better reason than that someday they may be the pastor of the driver of that car.

7. Text of Johann Heermann (1630); stanzas 1–3 of the translation by Robert S. Bridges (1899).

8. The English term "Maundy Thursday" has generated much confusion ("How can Thursday be a Monday?"). "Maundy" is probably a corruption of the Latin word *mandatum*—hence the English word "mandate," or commandment—and springs from the traditional use on this occasion of John 13:34 ("I give you a new commandment, that you love one another. Just as I have loved you, you also should love one another"). While John 13:1-17, 31*b*-35 is assigned in the lectionary for this day, the demise of Latin learning probably makes this explanation more trouble than it is worth. In England the custom arose of having this exhortation fulfilled by the presentation to a poor person of a gold coin on this day; the gift, presented by the monarch, is still known as the "maundy money" or simply "the maundy." This latter use, of course, simply adds to the confusion about what the title "Maundy Thursday" means.

9. See the *United Methodist Book of Worship* (Nashville: United Methodist Publishing House, 1992), pp. 354-61, with the translation by James H. Charlesworth. For an ample adaptation of the medieval service across three evenings, see *Holy Week Offices*, ed. Massey H. Shepherd, Jr. (Greenwich, Conn.: Seabury Press, 1958), pp. 27-71. A reduced version, intended for use on Wednesday evening only, appears in the *Book of Occasional Services* of The Episcopal Church (New York: Church Hymnal Corporation, 1991), pp. 73-90.

10. Early in my pastoral ministry, on this evening I attempted to instill in the congregation a sense of intense foreboding and sorrow. In groups of eleven, the people moved from the worship space into an adjacent social hall where they sat at a long table having thirteen seats. Two were unoccupied: one representing Jesus and the other Judas. After the meal was reenacted, communicants returned to the silent and dimly lit worship space to contemplate the death of Jesus. The difficulty was not that the service was ineffective but that it was phony. I was asking people to pretend they did not know how the story ends, or at least to ignore the consequences of that ending. My aim was psychological when it should have been theological. When we read the story backward, Thursday evening may be a bittersweet occasion, but the sweetness of the resurrection, about which we know fully well, must not be negated. It is primarily by knowing assuredly that resurrection follows death that we are able to pass through some of life's greatest difficulties with hope.

11. A generic form of the Vigil rite together with commentary is found in the *New Handbook of the Christian Year* by Hickman, Saliers, Stookey, and White (Nashville: Abingdon Press, 1992), pp. 191-209.

12. For a description of the design and use of the Paschal Candle, see n. 5 of chap. 6, p. 180.

13. The fair linen that covers the Table of the Lord often is a single piece of white fabric that extends nearly to the floor at both ends of the table, thus being eight or more feet in length. Piety has often seen this as representing the "winding sheet" or burial shroud of Jesus. (Compare the form of the Shroud of Turin.) Jesus, being raised from the dead, has no further use for a burial cloth, which by the resurrection is transformed into the covering of the church's festal table. Thus to vest the bare

table at this point in the service can be a visible reminder of the transformative power of the resurrection and an indication that the meal eaten here is primarily a celebrative banquet after the manner of Emmaus.

14. For a full discussion, see my *Baptism: Christ's Act in the Church* (Nashville: Abingdon Press, 1982), pp. 53-55.

15. A translation by John Mason Neale and others of a seventh- or eighth-century Latin text.

5. *Christmas: The Great Exchange*

1. Stanza 2 of "Break Forth, O Beauteous Heavenly Light" as it appears in the *United Methodist Hymnal* (Nashville: United Methodist Publishing House, 1989), no. 223. In virtually all other hymnals this hymn consists of only one stanza of a longer text written by Johann Rist in 1641. The Hymnal Revision Committee of The United Methodist Church in 1986 asked a British hymn writer, Fred Pratt Green, to write additional stanzas. Working from Friedrich Hofmann's translation into English of Rist's original eleven stanzas in German, Green produced stanzas 2 and 3 for the United Methodist book. © 1989 by Hope Publishing Co. All rights reserved. Used by permission.

2. There may be more to the lyrics than meets the eye. First, the entire text seems to be about the gift of life. Until illustrators interpreted "five golden rings" to mean five pieces of jewelry, probably what was intended were golden ring-necked pheasants. (Recall the pheasants on the roof of the stable in the depiction of the adoration of the Magi by Fra Angelico and Fra Filippo Lippi.) Thus the first seven gifts were all birds (which since ancient times have been symbols of the soul), and the other five gifts were all energetic human beings (we, once dead in our sins, have been given new life in Christ). "My true Love," of course, is intended to be God, not a paramour. Seven is that important sacred number of ancient Israel; five is also a significant biblical number (five books of Moses, for example) and often was taken to refer to the completeness of humanity, even as seven was taken to refer to the fullness of divinity.

Furthermore, the items separately had symbolic connotations when the text was devised. The partridge, for example, was a symbol of truth and of the church; and the pear tree represented the Incarnation and Christ's love for the church. (See entries for "partridge" and "pear" in sections I and II respectively of George Ferguson's *Signs and Symbols in Christian Art* [New York: Oxford University Press, 1958].) "Two turtledoves" were to remind Christians that when Jesus was presented in the temple, Mary, being a poor woman who could not afford to bring a sacrificial lamb, instead brought two turtledoves (Luke 2:24; Lev. 15:29). One further thing for the record: "Calling birds" actually is "colly birds"—blackbirds, not talking parrots or mynahs.

The nature of the repeated giving represents the outrageous generosity of God; indeed, the cumulative total of 364 gifts may be intended to suggest that God's provision for us extends to every day of the year. Misinterpretations and secularization of this old text in the recent revival of its use probably reveal more about our loss of theological awareness than we care to admit.

3. Here we who speak English fare a bit better than at Easter and Lent, when our terms have no obvious Christian connotation. Still, in many tongues what we call Christmas is more explicitly linked to the nativity: Latin, *Natalis*, birth, gave rise to the Italian *Natale*. In French, *Noël* also means birth. The German *Weihnachten* can

mean "night of inauguration" (of the incarnation) or "night of consecration" (either "holy night" generally, or with particular reference to the consecration of the Mass and thus closely related to our "Christmas").

4. In the United States regional differences are great. In contrast to Puritan-dominated New England, in Virginia the Cavaliers preserved many of the old English customs, which are retained or now recovered, particularly in Williamsburg. Where Scandinavians settled, St. Lucia's Day (December 13) is observed as the beginning of the season. Some Protestants of the Appalachian South still maintain "Old Christmas" in January following the old Julian calendar's calculations, because that was the calendar used in the British Isles before their ancestors migrated here. Everywhere the customs (and recipes) brought from other countries endure, even if in forms almost unrecognizable by the descendants of the immigrant peoples.

5. A few years ago the then senior bishop of my denomination (United Methodist) publicly stated that Christmas Eve Eucharists are singularly inappropriate. Why should we want to do something so sad at a time that is so happy, he wondered. Such a sentiment reveals a view of the sacrament, not as manifestation of the presence of the Risen One in our midst and of our perpetual thanksgiving, but as only a kind of funeral for the dying Jesus, appropriate primarily to Holy Week. Happily, that old, narrow Zwinglian-Protestant view is on the wane in most quarters.

6. An accessible adaptation is in the *United Methodist Book of Worship* (1992), pp. 284-88.

7. Attempts by the church to "kill Santa Claus" are probably futile. Instead of insisting that not even a picture of the jolly old man can appear anywhere on church property, we do better to interpret the process by which this hybrid character has come into being in the past century and a half. Although the development of Santa Claus as we know him is complex and involves the incorporation of cultural figures unrelated to Christianity, certainly there is a clear line of development back to the veneration of St. Nicholas, a fourth-century bishop of Myra in Asia Minor noted for his compassion and generosity. Exploring the relationship of Santa Claus to St. Nicholas (who is commemorated in the calendar on December 6) can be a fruitful way of dealing with the often ambiguous role of Santa Claus in church. Certainly the wrong resolution to the problem is exemplified by a piece of kitsch increasingly sold even in church gift shops: the depiction of Santa in red attire trimmed with white fur, kneeling in adoration before the holy infant in the manger. (I am not making this up. If you have not already gotten one, sooner or later you will receive a Christmas card depicting this dreadful piety!)

Relating Santa to Nicholas of Myra is also a way of critiquing the Nordic features of the North Pole resident. The historical Nicholas, having been born in what is now Turkey, undoubtedly had skin far darker than could today fit into the category "white." He was most likely more Asian-Semitic than European-Caucasian.

8. In the Eastern churches January 6 originated not as the end of something but as a festival of the birth and baptism of Jesus as a unit, for both were seen to proclaim Messiah's manifestation to the world. Gradually the nativity got separated out as a December 25 celebration. The differing historical developments in East and West are summarized by A. A. MacArthur's article, "Epiphany," in the *Westminster Dictionary of Worship*, ed. J. G. Davies (Philadelphia: Westminster Press, 1976), pp. 170-71. For later and more thorough discussion, see Thomas J. Talley's *Origins of the Liturgical Year* (New York: Pueblo Publishing Co., 1986).

The system of counting in the West becomes very elusive. In England, January 6 was called "Twelfth Day," but it is the twelfth day after December 25; if December 25 is included in the count, January 5 is the twelfth day of Christmas. The great festivities that accompanied this day in England were called "Twelfth Night" (hence the name of Shakespeare's rollicking play); that term is equally ambiguous and can be the evening preceding January 6 or the evening of January 6. Popular literature about the Epiphany reflects this imprecision and can therefore be quite confusing.

9. This is the first Sunday in January except in years when December 25 falls on a Monday. Then the Epiphany is commemorated on December 31. Herein is an oddity of the calendar. When Christmas is on a Monday, the time from the First Sunday in Advent through the Sunday of the Baptism, inclusive, is 36 days. But in all other years that time is 43 days. That is counter-intuitive; given the fact that Advent ranges from 22 to 28 days in length and Christmas Day to Baptism spans 14 to 20 days, one would expect a sliding scale also when the overall cycle is calculated. Instead the full cycle is 43 days long, six years out of seven.

10. In the early centuries, Christians were often in trouble with the Roman emperor, who, considering himself divine, ordered all loyal subjects to present an offering of incense before a statue of him. Failure to do so was deemed treasonous. Surely the mention of incense in Revelation 5:8 and 8:3-4 is a way of saying to those tempted to give incense to Caesar: "Only Jesus is Lord. Save your incense for heaven; don't squander it on a false god." In the Revelation 18:11-15, incense is mentioned as no longer having a market in mercantile Babylon (i.e., Rome); in other words the pretensions of Caesar will be unmasked.

11. Various hymns set forth these meanings, from the rather ponderous Victorian standard by John H. Hopkins, Jr., "We Three Kings," to the jaunty Puerto Rican carol of today, "Da Tierra Lejana Venimos," the first line translated by George K. Evans as "From a distant home the Savior we come seeking."

12. In the lectionary system, John 1:29-42 is used in Year A on the Sunday after the Baptism of the Lord. Although it can be imported into the Sunday of the Baptism itself, particularly in Year A its use the following week can be a way of reinforcing what occurred seven days earlier and of presenting it to those who were then absent.

13. For amplification of these themes see my *Baptism: Christ's Act in the Church* (Nashville: Abingdon, 1982), pp. 94-99. If this whole approach (known technically as typological exegesis) seems like some strange new invention, see Jean Daniélou's *The Bible and the Liturgy*, vol. 3 of the Liturgical Studies series (Notre Dame: University of Notre Dame Press, 1956), especially chaps. 2–4.

14. Mary is not only in the bad graces of ultra-Protestant types but also of some feminists. In the latter camp, she is seen as a passive, compliant person, particularly by virtue of the conception, in which she has no active role. But often the hermeneutical knife cuts both ways. The same text that can be read as being anti-feminist can be interpreted as even more severely anti-masculinist, since Joseph has not even a passive role in the virginal conception. In John's Gospel, on the other hand, Mary is very assertive at the Cana wedding feast.

15. Stanza 2 and part of stanza 3 of a text by Vincent Stucky Stratton Coles (with a fourth stanza by F. Bland Tucker), published under the title "Ye Who Claim the Faith of Jesus."

179

6. Advent: The End and the Beginning

1. It was not always thus, nor is it everywhere. Often the beginning of the liturgical calendar has coincided with the civil calendar. Thus in Greek Orthodoxy the year begins on September 1, following an old Greek calendar. (Significantly, however, the first text in the Orthodox book of liturgical texts is that for Easter Day). At the Reformation, Thomas Hooker stated that in England the liturgical year began on March 25, which was then also New Year's Day in the civil calendar (*Ecclesiastical Polity*, LXXVI). Curiously, in England as late as 1751, March 25 was regarded as New Year's Day, on the theological warrant that the civil year should mark the beginning of the incarnation, and March 25 is the Annunciation, hence, presumably the day on which Jesus was conceived! In some eras December 25 has marked the opening of the liturgical year.

Nor has Advent always begun the fourth Sunday before Christmas Day. In some places it has consisted of five or six Sundays, nor has it always begun on a Sunday. At one point it was deemed appropriate that Advent be a penitential season approximately equal to Lent in length, and so it was begun on November 11 (and dubbed "St. Martin's Lent" since that is the day of Martin of Tours in the calendar).

2. Despite widespread impressions to the contrary, the New Testament never uses the phrase "second coming," which seems to have arisen in the second century. There are unfortunate consequences to the term: By making such a clear separation between the first coming (at Bethlehem) and the final coming (at the end of time), we may readily overlook the way in which during the interim Christ comes to us continually by the power of the Holy Spirit, whose function is ever to make the Risen One present to us. It is better to speak of the final coming, the ultimate coming, or the coming in glory (the preferred New Testament form); hence, the term "second coming" will not again be used here.

3. Hymn text by Yasushige Imakoma, 1965. Translated by Nobuaki Hanaoka, 1983. © 1983 The United Methodist Publishing House. All rights reserved. Used by permission.

4. Text by Charles Wesley.

5. The so-called Christ Candle of the Advent wreath is in no way to be confused with the Paschal Candle lighted throughout the Great Fifty Days. Recently a few church supply houses have concocted a two-in-one candlestand designed to appeal to those who value economy above symbolism. This device acts as a single candle-stand for the Paschal Candle, but can have added to it a circular holder for four additional candles during Advent. Such an attempt to save money on candleholders results only in a great confusion of practice and meaning.

The Paschal Candle is normally lighted at every service during the Great Fifty Days and remains unlighted thereafter, but in a visible place to remind us that the resurrection celebration reverberates throughout the year. There are two exceptions. The Paschal Candle (which usually stands at the font except during the Fifty Days) is lighted whenever baptism is administered. On the day of the funeral of a baptized person, it stands lighted at the foot of the coffin. These uses outside the Easter season remind us that baptism is our enlightenment and promise of resurrection, and that Christ, our Light, precedes us in death to show the way to eternal life. This symbolic use should make evident the double problem introduced by the two-in-one candlestand: (1) When there is a baptism or funeral during Advent or Christmas, the Advent ring has to be removed in order to make the Paschal Candle evident. If the baptisms occur, as they should, during Sunday worship, what happens to the lighting of the Advent wreath on those days? (2) If the same candle is used for the Paschal Candle and the Christ Candle of Advent, the uniqueness of the Great Fifty Days and their relation to baptism and burial is destroyed. If two different kinds of candles are used, then the Paschal Candle as a symbol of the resurrection disappears whenever it is more convenient to be economical than symbolically consistent.

Note that the Christ Candle is at most only slightly larger than the four Advent candles and has no prescribed decoration. The Paschal Candle, by contrast, is significantly larger than any other candle ever used by the Church. Commonly it has inscribed near its base a Greek cross—four arms of equal length (which is also the Greek letter "chi," the first letter in the Greek word known to us as "Christ"). Above and below the cross, respectively, are the first and final letters of the Greek alphabet, the Alpha and Omega of the Revelation 22:13; within the four angles formed at the junctures of the cross bars are the four digits of the Year of our Lord in which the candle was lighted at the Vigil. Thus we are reminded that our current time is set within the context of the Risen Christ, who is the beginning and the end of all things. Often a stylized nail is inserted at the end of each arm of the cross and at the point of their intersection, representing the five wounds of the Crucified One, now made glorious by the resurrection.

6. Yes, yes, I know that page 54 of the *New Handbook of the Christian Year* suggests that the four candles represent expectation, proclamation, joy, and purity. Many things in that book were included on the basis of a vote by the four co-authors; and on that issue I lost the vote, 3-1.

7. The text provided here is my own. I worked from the Latin text, compared a variety of English translations, and tried to bring my own rendering into line with the wording of the *New Revised Standard Version* of the Bible so that textual allusions can be seen more clearly. Some points of conflict had to be resolved by personal preference. Regarding the fifth antiphon, for example, the NRSV of Malachi 4:2 reads "righteousness," but the Latin text uses "iusticia." "Justice" seems to me to be the more forceful rendering, despite the NRSV.

8. United Methodists, in particular, should not suppose the season is limited to *United Methodist Hymnal* selections 195-216, which refer largely to the historical coming at Bethlehem. The eschatological coming of the Lord is proclaimed in selections 714-34, and many of these are quite appropriate for Advent.

9. A form of this service is found in the *United Methodist Book of Worship*, pp. 263-65. Unfortunately, in that form sung texts are restricted to looking backward to the expectation of Messiah fulfilled at Bethlehem. Also included in the service should be sung texts about the return in glory and reign of the Lord. (See foregoing note.)

7. Ordinary and Extraordinary Time

1. During the past quarter century, the lectionary adaptations have greatly evolved with respect to how the system is actually set out for use. Earlier ambiguities and sources of confusion have been resolved by indicating Sundays in reference to calendar dates, either as the "Sunday between August 7 and 13 inclusive" or as the "Sunday closest to August 10." In the earlier system such an occasion was referred to simply as the "19th Sunday in Ordinary Time." As a result of this evolution, the sequence of first, second, third is no longer of such great importance. But "Ordinary Time" is still used as an overarching title.

2. Claus Westermann, *Blessing in the Bible and the Life of the Church,* trans. Keith Crim (Philadelphia: Fortress Press, 1978).

3. In the Eastern Church (there appropriately called "the metamorphosis"), this feast has been observed as an important festival since the fourth century; it began to be kept in the West in the ninth century, but without a fixed date until 1457. Then it was assigned to August 6 as a way of giving thanks for the defeat of the Turks by John Hunyadi and the Franciscan, Juan Capistrano, at Belgrade on August 6 of the previous year. Given the shakiness of this placement, moving the observance to the Sunday prior to Lent not only poses no problems but greatly strengthens the theological role of Transfiguration in the overall calendar.

4. In some churches similar occasions existed in the past, but at different locations within the calendar. The Roman Catholic Church formerly observed Christ the King on the last Sunday of October. The Methodist Church in the *Book of Worship* of 1945 designated the last Sunday of August as the "Festival of Christ the King," a day which inaugurated "Kingdomtide," a season stretching to the beginning of Advent; this Sunday was given its distinctive color (white) in contrast to the red Sundays after Pentecost and the green Sundays of the balance of Kingdomtide. However, the later liturgical books of The Methodist Church and its successor, The United Methodist Church, retained "Kingdomtide" without an inaugural Sunday appointed.

8. The Sanctoral Cycle: Resurrection Power in Human Lives

1. Opening lines of a text by Fred Pratt Green.

2. Increasingly in the popular media such persons are referred to as "cultural icons." Many seem to think the metaphor is drawn from the world of computers, without realizing that the computer designers borrowed it from the church. How ironic that both computer screen symbols and persons referred to as "cultural icons" are named for those sacred pictures of ancient origin that depict the saints, in order to keep utmost in the minds of the faithful the power of God in human lives.

3. Although at first it seems a confusion of terms to call the celebration of Bethlehem the "birth day of Jesus," while calling the date of death the "day of the saint's birth into eternity," there is a cogent theological rationale. Were his death on Calvary regarded as the day of Jesus' birth into eternity, this would be in serious conflict with the historic affirmation concerning the preexistence of the Christ. Hence what appears at first an oddity is, in fact, an affirmation of what we have called "the great exchange." The One who is infinite and eternal was born into this temporal world so that we who are finite and temporal might be born into eternity.

4. An excellent resource not officially sanctioned (but not opposed) by denominational legislation is now available for United Methodists. Edited by Clifton F. Guthrie and entitled *For All the Saints: A Calendar of Commemorations for United Methodists,* it is available from the Order of Saint Luke Publications, P.O. Box 22279, Akron, OH 44302-0079. Far from being merely a calendar, it provides brief biographical commentaries concerning nearly two hundred persons. It is intended primarily for use in personal devotions; but this work and works like it are rich resources for teaching, including during "children's sermons," as suggested in this chapter.

5. Stanzas 1 and 3 of a text by Lesbia Scott, given here in the slightly altered form found in the *United Methodist Hymnal* of 1989.

6. Stanzas 1 and 2, followed by the first half of stanza 3 and the final half of stanza 4 of a Charles Wesley text.

7. Cited without further attribution by Susan Cahill, ed., in *Women and Fiction 2: Short Stories by and About Women* (New York and Scarborough, Ontario: Times Mirror, 1978; Mentor/New American Library), p. 67.

8. Terry Waite, *Taken on Trust* (New York, San Diego, London: Harcourt Brace & Co., 1993), p. 250.

Appendix 1: Putting Liturgical Colors in Their Place

1. *Symbols of the Church*, ed. Carroll E. Whittemore (Boston: Whittemore Associates, 1957), p. 20.

FOR FURTHER READING

Calendar centers largely on theological meaning and parish practice in relation to liturgical time; almost no attention is given to detailed historical development, much of which is exceedingly complex in its origins and technical in its detail. For such background see particularly Thomas J. Talley's *The Origins of the Liturgical Year* (New York: Pueblo Publishing Co., 1986). Talley traces emerging traditions in the early centuries and indicates how varying strands of calendrical practice were woven together. Also useful is Adolf Adam's *The Liturgical Year: Its History and Its Meaning After the Reform of the Liturgy* (New York: Pueblo Press, 1981; published originally in German in 1979). "Reform of the Liturgy" in the subtitle alludes specifically to the revision of the Roman Catholic rites after Vatican II. The relatively constricted approach suggested by that subtitle should not deter Protestant readers, however. The widespread use of a common three-year lectionary makes Adam's observations valuable across the spectrum of Western Christianity. Marion J. Hatchett's *Sanctifying Life, Time, and Space: An Introduction to Liturgical Study* (New York: Seabury Press, 1976) also provides helpful information in the sections entitled "The Sanctification of Time," found with each of its nine divisions.

Works written earlier than these three should be looked at more critically; much of the older historical scholarship has been superseded both by recent research and by the changes already noted that spring from lectionary revision. An old standard to consult in the light of this warning is A. Allan McArthur's *The Evolution of the Christian Year* (London: SCM Press, 1953).

Recent liturgical dictionaries hold a wealth of information, but it must be ferreted out, article by article, and there is no uniformity as to how the material is organized and listed. Peter E. Fink, S.J., has edited *The New Dictionary of Sacramental Worship* (Collegeville, Minn.: Liturgical Press, 1990); again the orientation is Roman Catholic but Protestants will find much that is helpful. The lack of running heads on each page can make the use of this book annoying, since some articles are many pages long. This problem can be alleviated by looking at the complete list of articles in the table of contents and noting which seem likely to bear upon the liturgical calendar, as well as by seeing the entry "Liturgical Time" on page 1343 of the Index. From the Protestant side, a book of similar design, but with briefer articles, is *The Westminster Dictionary of Worship*, edited by J. G. Davies (Philadelphia: Westminster Press, 1979); originally it was published in England by SCM Press in 1972 under the title *A Dictionary of Liturgy and Worship*. Because most of the articles on the calendar were written by Allan A. McArthur, a shortcut to finding the pertinent material is to look under his name in the list of contributors at the front of the book.

Robert F. Webber has edited *The Complete Library of Christian Worship* (Nashville: Star Song Publishing Group, 1994) in seven volumes (eight, actually, since volume 4 is in two books). Alas, each book has its own table of contents and index, with no omnibus index available. Most of the pertinent material is in volume 5, "The Services of the Christian Year," which sets forth actual patterns and practices. A wide variety of authors representing various traditions is used, with results that are generally excellent but with some unevenness in quality. A more ample bibliography than can be found here is supplied on pages 97-104 of volume 5.

For preachers who use the lectionary, *Social Themes of the Christian Year*, edited by Dieter H. Hessel, is a great help (Philadelphia: Geneva Press, 1983). All who preach on the passion, death, and resurrection will benefit from David Buttrick's *The Mystery and the Passion: A Homiletic Reading of the Gospel Traditions* (Minneapolis: Fortress Press, 1992). An older work for use by those who have a Barthian bent is *Preaching Through the Christian Year: A Selection of Exegetical Passages from the Church Dogmatics of Barth*, edited by John McTavish and Harold Wells (Grand Rapids: Wm. B. Eerdmans Publishing Co., 1978).

Both preachers and worship planners will find rich theological insights in Reginald H. Fuller's *Preaching the Lectionary* (Collegeville, Minn.: Liturgical Press, 1984) originally published by the same press in 1974 as *Preaching the New Lectionary*. Fuller often comments on the nature of the liturgical occasion itself; hence, even those who do not preach (or do not use the lectionary but nevertheless observe the Year in its current form) will benefit from consulting this work. A multivolume set of lectionary commentaries that has much the same benefit (*Preaching the Revised Common Lectionary*) was issued over three years for the lectionary cycle that began in Advent 1992. Its authors, Marion Soards, Thomas Dozeman, and Kendall McCabe, gave particular attention to liturgical meaning and observance (Nashville: Abingdon Press, 1992–94).

A single-volume set of resources that I cowrote with Hoyt L. Hickman, Don E. Saliers, and James F. White is *The New Handbook of the Christian Year* (Abingdon Press, 1992); the original version was published in 1986 under the title *The Handbook of the Christian Year*. Many of its suggested forms and practices have made their way into *The United Methodist Book of Worship* (Nashville: United Methodist Publishing House, 1992); and the book you have in your hand greatly amplifies its underlying theological assumptions. But the *Handbook* may still be useful to lectionary users for its week-by-week suggestions concerning hymns and related materials.

In any given year, a plethora of liturgical resources becomes available; but let the buyer beware. Some of these are not of high quality theologically, liturgically, or both. A few authors still produce resources that regard Lent as six-and-a-half weeks of Good Friday–like observances, broken in solemnity only by a Palm Sunday celebration that is utterly joyous. There are writers who think that Advent continues to be a heavily penitential season, or, alternatively, that Advent is simply Christmas-come-early. Browse carefully before buying.

Despite the jokes about a camel being a horse put together by a committee, materials produced by denominational liturgical committees (and persons who have served on them) are most trustworthy; whatever its faults, the committee process provides a pooling of wisdom and reins in the more excessive approaches to which individual writers may be prone. Liturgy, after all, is a corporate event; forms that may be quite appropriate for certain individuals praying in solitude sometimes do not work well in a community at prayer. Denominational liturgy books are sensitive to this distinction. An additional bonus: Because denominational worship books are sold by the hundreds of thousands (or even millions) the price per copy is low. On a small budget you can accumulate a shelf filled with the recent materials of the Episcopalians, Lutherans, United Methodists, United Presbyterians, and others.

Non-Catholics are usually astonished to learn (because it so destroys our stereotypes of a monolithic church) that, unlike Protestant groups, the Roman Catholic Church has no official denominational publishing house; it relies on an entrepreneurial free-market system. There is not even such a thing as an official Roman Catholic hymnal. Since many Catholic-oriented materials are either fully ecumenical in spirit, or readily adapted by Protestants, it is useful to check the resource catalogs of groups such as The Liturgical Press of Collegeville, MN 56321, and Liturgy Training Publications, 1800 North Hermitage Avenue, Chicago, IL 60622.

An ecumenical organization with a specific focus on liturgical resources and an excellent track for quality is The Liturgical Conference, 8750 Georgia Avenue, Silver Spring, MD 20910-3621. Each issue of its quarterly subscription publication, *Liturgy*, centers on a particular topic addressed from diverse perspectives. Some back-issues are available for purchase separately. Issue titles have included "All Saints Among the Churches," "The Calendar," "The Christmas Cycle," "Easter's Fifty Days," and "From Ashes to Fire," a book of resources for Lent-Easter.

Finally, there are many voluntary organizations for those interested in worship. These groups have local chapters as well as regional and national networks. Some are specifically denominational while others are intentionally ecumenical. Many send newsletters or even journals to their members and are an excellent source of up-to-date information. Even persons who cannot attend organizational meetings may regularly find benefits far beyond the cost of their annual dues payment.

INDEX

187